WOOD STRUCTURE AND IDENTIFICATION

SYRACUSE WOOD SCIENCE SERIES, 6
Wilfred A. Côté, *Editor*

 SYRACUSE WOOD SCIENCE SERIES
Wilfred A. Côté, *Editor*

WOOD
STRUCTURE AND IDENTIFICATION

H.A. CORE, W.A. CÔTÉ, and A.C. DAY

SYRACUSE UNIVERSITY PRESS   1976

Library of Congress Cataloging in Publication Data
Core, Harold A
  Wood structure and identification.

  (Syracuse wood science series; 6)
  Bibliography: p.
  Includes index.
    1. Wood—Identification.   2. Wood—Anatomy—Atlases.
  3. Timber—North America—Identification.   I.   Côté,
  Wilfred A., joint author.   II.   Day, A. C., joint author.
  III.   Title.   IV.   Series.
  SD536.C67   674'.12   76-26938
  ISBN 0-8156-5041-8
  ISBN 0-8156-5042-6 pbk.

Manufactured in the United States of America

THIS BOOK IS DEDICATED TO STUDENTS, COLLEAGUES, AND OTHERS WHO SHARE WITH US A DEEP AND HUMBLE APPRECIATION OF THE BEAUTY, THE VALUE, AND THE MYSTERY OF WOOD.

Harold A. Core, presently of the University of Tennessee, Wilfred A. Côté, and Arnold C. Day worked together for fifteen years at SUNY College of Environmental Science and Forestry at Syracuse, where Dr. Côté is Professor of Wood Technology, Director of the N. C. Brown Center for Ultrastructure Studies, and Editor of the Syracuse Wood Science Series.

CONTENTS

PREFACE

Wood as a material currently holds particular interest among crafts-men and hobbyists, though it has been appreciated by others in furniture, as construction material, and as an art medium for cen-turies. Those who use or work with wood often want to learn more about its unique composition, structure, and identification through curiosity as well as a desire to utilize it more effectively.

The subject of wood structure and identification is treated widely in a number of references and textbooks, but most of them are not recent and the newer ones are published in foreign lan-guages. Also, the better works in English cover more than the structure of wood and the identification of woods native to North America; they include many subjects which are of interest primar-ily to wood technologists—ultrastructure, the chemical nature of the wood cell wall, and the mechanical or physical properties of wood.

In our opinion there is a need for a book that is more limited in scope than a wood technology textbook. The forestry student who should know something about wood structure and be able to identify native woods—but not necessarily be a specialist in all phases of wood science—could use such a manual. The teacher of woodworking or shop in high school or junior college likely will find this format better suited to his needs or those of his students. The many individuals and concerns utilizing wood in making furni-ture, carving, sculpture, and hobby activities have a need for this approach.

Emphasis has been placed on illustrating features of wood structure more clearly than in any other book on wood iden-tification. A special effort was made to produce new photomic-rographs that represent the structure one sees with a light microscope without unusual skills. Given a hand lens and a

microscope, the essentials of wood structure and wood identification may be learned with the aid of this manual. Not only are the
illustrations and descriptions designed for self-teaching, but the
appendices include supporting material on the preparation of temporary microscope slides and on other techniques to which the
reader can refer if teacher instruction is not employed. The keys for
identification of softwoods and hardwoods represent decades of
experience in selecting consistent features for accurate analysis.

The title of this manual suggests that wood structure is the
first topic covered and then wood identification. Naturally it is
essential that a minimum background in wood structure be developed before structural features can be used to determine the
source of the wood in question. To make wood structure more
realistic, the three-dimensional perspective offered by scanning
electron microscopy was used in the preparation of a large number
of photographs. When prepared with a scanning electron microscope (SEM) the photographs are called scanning electron micrographs. While this technique is not new to wood science, to our
knowledge it has never been employed in a book designed for use
at this level. The micrographs have been labeled to help identify
quickly and easily those structural details most readily commu-
nicated through visual aids.

For the sake of brevity, we have taken one liberty in preparing this manual. The names of the authors have been omitted from
scientific names. A footnote to Table 1 details this departure from
the practice followed by most botanists. We believe that the list of
references will provide sufficient sources for those who must use a
complete scientific name.

The spelling of the common names of the trees listed in
Tables 1 and 2 follows that given in the *Check List of Native and
Naturalized Trees of the United States (Including Alaska)*. Hyphenation is used when the name employed is not a correct species
name. For example, yellow-poplar is not a true poplar and Osage-
orange is not a true orange tree. The names applied to commercial
lumber do not always agree with the common names of the trees,
and hyphenation is used infrequently. The same commercial
lumber name may be applied to several distinct species. The
lumber name has been used in the Identification Keys and in
Appendix D.

Whether you are a student or a teacher, young or old, we
hope that this guide will introduce you to the mysteries and joys of
the knowledge of wood, a remarkable material.

Knoxville, Tennessee   H. A. CORE
Syracuse, New York   W. A. CÔTÉ
May 1, 1976   A. C. DAY

WOOD STRUCTURE AND IDENTIFICATION

What Is Wood?

INTRODUCTION

Wood is the cell wall material produced by cells of the cambium in a living tree. In its commercial form, such as lumber, the individual wood cells are dead and the original protoplasmic cell content has largely disappeared. Wood cells make up the xylem portion of the tree as contrasted with the phloem (bark), which forms the protective outer layer and is generally discarded in the production of wood products. Both the xylem and the phloem have their origin in the cambial zone, a thin initiating layer of living cells sandwiched between the two (Figure 1). During the growing season the cells of the cambium divide frequently into so-called daughter cells which may themselves subdivide immediately or differentiate into specialized elements of the bark or the wood portion of the tree trunk.

The terms "softwood" and "hardwood" are commonly employed in the trade, but they can be confusing because some softwoods are hard, while many hardwoods are soft. Softwood lumber is derived from logs of coniferous trees (conifers of the Gymnosperms), and hardwood is the product of broad-leaved species (Dicotyledons of the Angiosperms). Most of the wood marketed in North America is derived from the stem or trunk of these two major categories of trees. Monocotyledons produce large quantities of material, namely bamboo, but the vascular tissue is scattered in bundles throughout the stem. Lumber for our domestic market cannot be manufactured from bamboo.

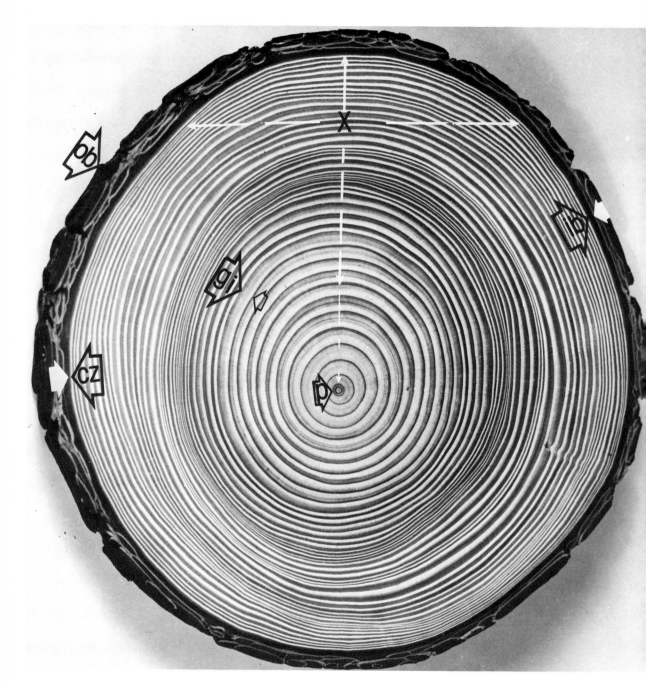

Figure 1. Cross-section of the woody stem of a conifer, Douglas-fir, *Pseudotsuga menziesii,* showing the following: cz = cambial zone; p = pith; gi = growth increment or growth ring; x = xylem or wood; ob = outer dead bark or outer dead phloem; and ib = inner living bark or inner living phloem.

Gymnosperms are of very ancient lineage, extending back through the Carboniferous period into the Devonian, at least three hundred million years. At the present time the seven orders of Gymnosperms have been reduced to four living orders: Cycadales, Ginkgoales, Coniferales, and Gnetales. The other three are found only in fossil form. Of the four living orders of Gymnosperms, only Coniferales is represented on the commercial market. Samples of *Ginkgo biloba* (Ginkgoales) might be found, but it is generally grown as an ornamental tree, not for timber. Neither Cycadales nor Gnetales produces wood suitable for lumber.

Depending on the classification scheme one prefers to follow, the Coniferales may be divided into four families or seven families. About five hundred species are recognized and they are classified into fifty-one genera. Seventeen of the genera are found in the United States and may be divided into four families if the seven-family scheme is used. Among these genera there are approximately fifty timber species in this country (Table 1).

Table 1

CONIFEROUS TIMBER TREES OF THE UNITED STATES		
Family and Species*	Commercial Lumber	Tree Name
PINACEAE		
*Pinus strobus**	northern white pine	eastern white pine
Pinus monticola	Idaho white pine	western white pine
Pinus lambertiana	sugar pine	sugar pine

*Scientific names, shown in Tables 1 and 2 in italic type, follow the binomial system of nomenclature and are written in Latin so that they can be used and understood universally. In a strict botanical sense, the scientific name for a tree consists of three elements: the genus (generic name), which is capitalized; the species name, which is not; and the author's name (the person who named and described it), which is generally abbreviated.

In this manual the authors' names have been omitted for brevity. However, the complete scientific name for any tree or wood referred to in this manual may be found in the *Check List* mentioned in the first footnote, above. This publication, by Elbert L. Little, Jr., includes many other items of information as well such as common names, derivations of scientific names, and the range where the tree can be found.

As an example in the use of scientific and common names, the tree eastern white pine is the source of northern white pine lumber. Its scientific name is *Pinus strobus* L. It was named by Linnaeus. Note that the common names of trees are not capitalized unless a proper noun is used in the name as in the case of Utah juniper.

Table 1

CONIFEROUS TIMBER TREES OF THE UNITED STATES		
Family and Species	Commercial Lumber	Tree Name
Pinus banksiana	jack pine	jack pine
Pinus contorta	lodgepole pine	lodgepole pine
Pinus resinosa	Norway pine, red pine	red pine
Pinus ponderosa	ponderosa pine; western yellow pine	ponderosa pine
Pinus jeffreyi [†]	Jeffrey pine; western yellow pine	Jeffrey pine
Pinus taeda	southern yellow pine	loblolly pine
Pinus palustris	southern yellow pine	longleaf pine
Pinus rigida	southern yellow pine	pitch pine
Pinus echinata	southern yellow pine	shortleaf pine
Pinus elliottii	southern yellow pine	slash pine
Pinus virginiana	southern yellow pine	Virginia pine
Picea glauca	eastern spruce	white spruce
Picea mariana	eastern spruce	black spruce
Picea rubens	eastern spruce	red spruce
Picea engelmannii	Engelman spruce	Engelman spruce
Picea pungens	Engelman spruce	blue spruce
Picea sitchensis	Sitka spruce	Sitka spruce
Larix laricina	eastern larch	tamarack
Larix occidentalis	western larch	western larch
Pseudotsuga menziesii	Douglas-fir	Douglas-fir
Abies balsamea	balsam fir; eastern fir	balsam fir
Abies fraseri	balsam fir	Fraser fir
Abies grandis	white fir	grand fir
Abies procera	white fir; noble fir	noble fir

† Species of secondary importance are indented.

Table 1 (continued)

CONIFEROUS TIMBER TREES OF THE UNITED STATES

Family and Species	Commercial Lumber	Tree Name
Abies amabilis	white fir	Pacific silver fir
Abies concolor	white fir	white fir
Tsuga canadensis	eastern hemlock	eastern hemlock
Tsuga caroliniana	eastern hemlock	Carolina hemlock
Tsuga mertensiana	mountain hemlock	mountain hemlock
Tsuga heterophylla	western hemlock	west coast hemlock
(CUPRESSACEAE)		
Chamaecyparis nootkatensis	Alaska cedar	Alaska-cedar
Chamaecyparis lawsoniana	Port Orford cedar	Port-Orford-cedar
Chamaecyparis thyoides	southern white cedar	Atlantic white-cedar
Juniperus virginiana	eastern red cedar	eastern red cedar
Juniperus silicicola	eastern red cedar	southern red cedar
Juniperus deppeana	western juniper	alligator juniper
Juniperus scopulorum	western juniper	Rocky Mountain juniper
Juniperus osteosperma	western juniper	Utah juniper
Juniperus occidentalis	western juniper	western juniper
Libocedrus decurrens	incense cedar	incense-cedar
Thuja occidentalis	northern white cedar	northern white-cedar
Thuja plicata	western red cedar	western red cedar
(TAXODIACEAE)		
Taxodium distichum	cypress	baldcypress

(   ) The conservative classification system of Dalla Torre and Harms is followed by the U. S. Forest Service as published in the *Check List of Native and Naturalized Trees of the United States (Including Alaska)*, Agriculture Handbook No. 41 (1953). In this system, the families Pinaceae, Cupressaceae, and Taxodiaceae are combined into the Pinaceae. In the above listing the families are shown separately for convenience.

Table 1 (continued)

CONIFEROUS TIMBER TREES OF THE UNITED STATES		
Family and Species	Commercial Lumber	Tree Name
Taxodium distichum *var. nutans*	cypress	pondcypress
Sequoia sempervirens *Sequoia gigantea*	redwood	redwood giant sequoia
TAXACEAE		
Taxus brevifolia	Yew, Pacific yew	Pacific yew

Angiosperms are considered to be of more recent origin than gymnosperms. Hardwood fossils have been found from as far back as the Jurassic period which is at least 160 million years ago. Among the dicotyledons there are tens of thousands of species, but not all are trees. There are approximately eight hundred species of hardwoods in the United States, while in the tropics there are many thousands. Those species found in this country can be assigned to approximately twenty-three families and the eight hundred species may be reduced to perhaps fifty important commercial woods (Table 2).

Table 2

HARDWOOD TIMBER TREES OF THE UNITED STATES		
Family and Species*	Commercial Lumber	Tree Name
ACERACEAE		
Acer saccharum	hard maple	sugar maple
Acer nigrum	hard maple	black maple

* Species of secondary importance are indented.

Table 2 (continued)

HARDWOOD TIMBER TREES OF THE UNITED STATES

Family and Species	Commercial Lumber	Tree Name
Acer rubrum	soft maple	red maple
Acer saccharinum	soft maple	silver maple
Acer macrophyllum	Oregon maple	bigleaf maple
Acer negundo	box elder	boxelder
AQUIFOLIACEAE		
Ilex opaca	holly	American holly
BETULACEAE		
Alnus rubra	red alder	red alder
Betula alleghaniensis	birch	yellow birch
Betula lenta	birch	sweet birch
Betula nigra	birch	river birch
Betula papyrifera	birch	paper birch
Betula populifolia	birch	gray birch
Carpinus caroliniana	blue beech	American hornbeam
Ostrya virginiana	ironwood	eastern hophornbeam
BIGNONIACEAE		
Catalpa bignonioides	catalpa	southern catalpa
Catalpa speciosa	catalpa	northern catalpa
CORNACEAE		
Cornus florida	dogwood	flowering dogwood
Cornus nuttalli	dogwood	Pacific dogwood

Table 2 (continued)

HARDWOOD TIMBER TREES OF THE UNITED STATES

Family and Species	Commercial Lumber	Tree Name
Nyssa aquatica	tupelo	water tupelo
Nyssa ogeche	tupelo	Ogeechee tupelo
Nyssa sylvatica	tupelo (black gum)	black tupelo
EBENACEAE		
Diospyros virginiana	persimmon	common persimmon
ERICACEAE		
Arbutus menziesii	madrone	Pacific madrone
Oxydendron arboreum	sourwood	sourwood
FAGACEAE		
Castanea dentata	chestnut	American chestnut
Castanopsis chrysophylla	golden chinkapin	golden chinkapin
Fagus grandifolia	beech	American beech
Lithocarpus densiflorus	tan oak	Tanoak
Quercus rubra	red oak	northern red oak
Quercus falcata	red oak	southern red oak
Quercus velutina	red oak	black oak
Quercus shumardii	red oak	Shumard oak
Quercus falcata var pagodaefolia	red oak	cherrybark oak
Quercus laurifolia	red oak	laurel oak
Quercus marilandica	red oak	blackjack oak
Quercus kelloggii	red oak	California black oak
Quercus ellipsoidalis	red oak	northern pin oak
Quercus palustris	red oak	pin oak
Quercus coccinea	red oak	scarlet oak
Quercus laevis	red oak	turkey oak
Quercus phellos	red oak	willow oak
Quercus nuttallii	red oak	Nuttall oak

Table 2 (continued)

HARDWOOD TIMBER TREES OF THE UNITED STATES

Family and Species	Commercial Lumber	Tree Name
Quercus alba	white oak	white oak
Quercus prinus	white oak	chestnut oak
Quercus michauxii	white oak	swamp chestnut oak
Quercus bicolor	white oak	swamp white oak
Quercus stellata	white oak	post oak
Quercus douglasii	white oak	blue oak
Quercus macrocarpa	white oak	bur oak
Quercus emoryi	white oak	Emory oak
Quercus garryana	white oak	overcup oak
Quercus gambelii	white oak	Oregon white oak
Quercus arizonica	white oak	Arizona white oak
Quercus lobata	white oak	California white oak
Quercus virginiana	white oak	live oak

HAMAMELIDACEAE

Liquidambar styraciflua	gum, sap gum, red gum	sweet gum

HIPPOCASTANACEAE

Aesculus octandra	buckeye	yellow buckeye
Aesculus glabra	buckeye	Ohio buckeye

JUGLANDACEAE

Carya ovata	hickory	shagbark hickory
Carya glabra	hickory	pignut hickory
Carya tomentosa	hickory	mockernut hickory
Carya laciniosa	hickory	shellbark hickory
Carya cordiformis	pecan	bitternut hickory
Carya illinoensis	pecan	pecan
Carya myristicaeformis	pecan	nutmeg hickory
Carya aquatica	pecan	water hickory

Table 2 (continued)

HARDWOOD TIMBER TREES OF THE UNITED STATES

Family and Species	Commercial Lumber	Tree Name
Juglans cinerea	butternut	butternut
Juglans nigra	walnut	black walnut
Juglans major	walnut	California walnut
LAURACEAE		
Persea borbonia	red bay	redbay
Sassafras albidum	sassafras	sassafras
Umbellularia californica	Oregon-myrtle	California-laurel
LEGUMINOSAE		
Cercis canadensis	redbud	redbud
Cladrastis lutea	yellow wood	yellowwood
Gleditsia triacanthos	honey locust	honeylocust
Gymnocladus dioicus	Kentucky coffee tree	Kentucky coffeetree
Robinia pseudoacacia	locust	black locust
MAGNOLIACEAE		
Liriodendron tulipifera	poplar	yellow-poplar
Magnolia acuminata	cucumber	cucumbertree
Magnolia grandiflora	magnolia	southern magnolia
Magnolia virginiana	magnolia	sweetbay

Table 2 (continued)

HARDWOOD TIMBER TREES OF THE UNITED STATES

Family and Species	Commercial Lumber	Tree Name
MORACEAE		
Maclura pomifera	Osage orange	Osage-orange
Morus rubra	mulberry	red mulberry
OLEACEAE		
Fraxinus americana	white ash	white ash
Fraxinus pennsylvanica	white ash	green ash
Fraxinus nigra	black ash	black ash
Fraxinus latifolia	Oregon ash	Oregon ash
Fraxinus profunda	pumpkin ash	pumpkin ash
Fraxinus quadrangulata	white ash	blue ash
PLATANACEAE		
Platanus occidentalis	sycamore	American sycamore
RHAMNACEAE		
Rhamnus purshiana	buckthorn	cascara buckthorn
Rhamnus caroliniana	buckthorn	Carolina buckthorn
STYRACACEAE		
Halesia carolina	silverbell	Carolina silverbell

Table 2   (continued)

HARDWOOD TIMBER TREES OF THE UNITED STATES

Family and Species	Commercial Lumber	Tree Name
ROSACEAE		
Cercocarpus ledifolius	mountain mahogany	curlleaf cercocarpus
Prunus serotina	cherry	black cherry
SALICACEAE		
Populus deltoides	cottonwood	eastern cottonwood
Populus balsamifera	cottonwood	balsam cottonwood
Populus sargentii	cottonwood	plains cottonwood
Populus heterophylla	cottonwood	swamp cottonwood
Populus trichocarpa	cottonwood	black cottonwood
Populus tremuloides	aspen	quaking aspen
Populus grandidentata	aspen	bigtooth aspen
Salix nigra	willow	black willow
Salix amygdaloides	willow	peachleaf willow
TILIACEAE		
Tilia americana	basswood	American basswood
Tilia heterophylla	basswood	white basswood
ULMACEAE		
Celtis occidentalis	hackberry	hackberry
Celtis laevigata	hackberry	sugarberry
Ulmus americana	soft elm	American elm
Ulmus rubra	soft elm	slippery elm

Table 2 (continued)

HARDWOOD TIMBER TREES OF THE UNITED STATES

Family and Species	Commercial Lumber	Tree Name
Ulmus thomasii	rock elm	rock elm
Ulmus crassifolia	rock elm	cedar elm
Ulmus serotina	rock elm	September elm
Ulmus alata	rock elm	winged elm

NATURALIZED SPECIES

BIGNONIACEAE

Paulownia tomentosa	Paulownia	royal paulownia

MELIACEAE

Melia azedarach	Chinaberry	Chinaberry

SIMARUBACEAE

Ailanthus altissima	Ailanthus	Ailanthus

LEGUMINOSAE

Albizia julibrissin	mimosa	silktree

CHARACTERISTICS OF WOOD

Even with the unaided eye, there are structural features of wood that can be recognized easily and provide useful evidence for the identification of wood species. The basic ones are considered here after first establishing some simple ground rules on perspective.

Planes of Wood

When discussing structural features of wood it is useful to designate which surface is being referred to. Three distinctive planes exposing different views of wood structure can be noted. First, a transverse or cross-section is produced by cutting across the stem perpendicularly. Growth increments, wood rays, sapwood-heartwood boundaries, all described in detail below, can be viewed on the cross-section of a tree trunk.

Second, a radial surface is created by cutting longitudinally from the center of the stem (the pith) to the bark. The same features listed above can be seen on the radial surface, although their appearance will be quite different from this aspect. Third, a cut in a plane tangential to the bark and perpendicular to the wood rays reveals a tangential surface. The ends of the wood rays can be observed on this surface, but the successive growth increments and the contrast between sapwood and heartwood are not as apparent. Figures 2, 4, and 5 should be helpful in the recognition of these three surface views and in an understanding of their interrelationships. Without this concept it is difficult to describe the more detailed anatomical features which distinguish one wood species from another.

Growth Increments

Generally it is possible to recognize the delineation between growth increments or annual growth rings on the cross-section because of a change in pattern of cell distribution or a change in cell size as the year's growth proceeds (Figures 1, 3, and 4). In the temperate zones, where such increments reflect one year's growth, it is possible to estimate the age of a tree by counting the number of rings produced from the center of the stem to the cambium at the periphery of the xylem. Under tropical conditions, growth cycles may be affected by wet and dry seasons rather than annual dormancy period, thus injecting possible confusion into an estimate if two or more cycles occur in a single year. Under uniform growing conditions, no differences may occur.

Figure 2. Planes of wood and their usual designation:

X = Transverse surface or cross-section; R = radial surface (quartered); T = tangential surface (flat or plain surface).

In many woods the effect of seasonal growth responses results in characteristic patterns within the growth increment. For example, the cells produced at the beginning of the growing season may be quite different from those produced later; cell walls may become thicker, cell dimensions reduced, or cell types changed. In conifers, the tracheids (cells) produced in the spring are large and thin-walled in most cases. As the growing season progresses, there may be a gradual change in cell size and cell wall thickness or it may be very abrupt. In the first instance the transition is classed as gradual (Figure 3) while in the second case it would be called an abrupt transition (Figure 4). These are structural characteristics that are helpful in separating one wood from another.

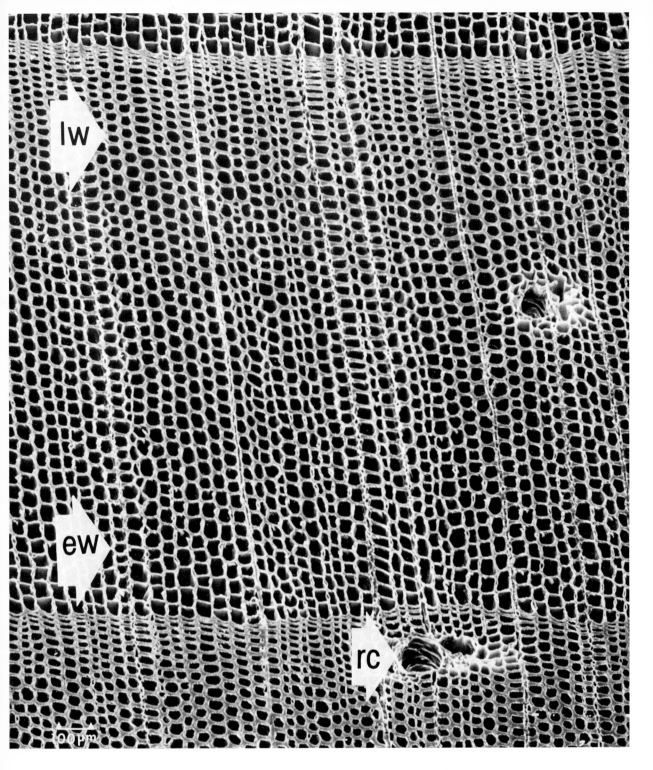

Figure 3. Gradual transition in a coniferous wood, eastern white pine, *Pinus strobus*. Tracheid size changes gradually from earlywood (ew) to latewood (lw). Note the longitudinal resin canals (rc) on this transverse surface. Scanning electron micrograph (SEM).

Figure 4. Abrupt transition in a coniferous wood, red pine, *Pinus resinosa*. Tracheid size changes abruptly from earlywood (ew) to latewood (lw). Note the resin canals (rc) on the transverse surface and the ray (r) on the radial surface. Scanning electron micrograph.

The same phenomenon may be observed in hardwoods but, due to a difference in cellular composition, the effect is somewhat different. Hardwoods are also known as porous woods because of the pores which are visible on the transverse surface. Pores are cross-sections of vessels which are large thin-walled structures made up of individual cells called vessel elements or vessel segments (Figures 5, 7, and 9). Vessel segments are joined end-to-end and extend vertically for long distances as vessels are specialized for conduction. Vessels are not found in softwoods.

In "earlywood," that is, the wood formed early in the growing season, the vessels are often very large in diameter. As the season progresses there may be an abrupt change into production of much smaller vessels in some woods. The term "ring-porous" is used in describing these porous woods (Figure 16a). Other species may have the same size pores distributed throughout the growth increment and these would be classed as "diffuse-porous" woods (Figure 16c). Since hardwoods are complex in structure it is to be expected that some species would not fit either category and the terms "semi-ring-porous" or "semi-diffuse-porous" may be applied (Figure 16b).

The term "latewood" refers to the portion of the annual increment produced late in the growing season. Because of significant differences between the latewood of one growth ring and the earlywood of the next growth ring, in ring-porous and semi-ring-porous woods the boundary separating the two years of wood production is generally quite distinct. In some species, including the diffuse-porous woods, there is a row of terminal cells produced, thus accentuating this dividing line.

Although it may not be immediately obvious, a tree tapers like a cone from base to top. Therefore a tree, especially of the coniferous species, can be represented as a series of elongated, thin, hollow cones of wood layers. Each layer consists of a growth increment produced in a single year and each layer encloses or overlaps the preceding one. If a cut is made through a tree stem several feet above the ground, some of the cones produced when the tree was very young would not appear and a count of growth rings would yield an incorrect age for the tree. It follows that the layers produced even when the tree was but a seedling must be counted to arrive at a relatively accurate age estimate.

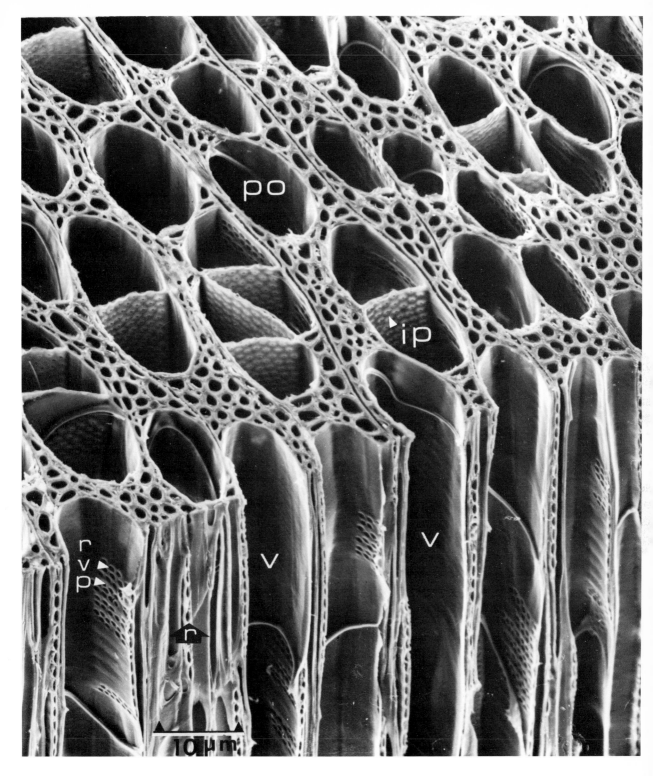

Figure 5. Scanning electron micrograph of a hardwood, *Populus deltoides*, showing vessels (v), the characteristic structural feature of the wood of broadleaved species. Note also the inter-vessel pitting (ip), ray-vessel pitting (rvp), and the pores (po) which are vessels as seen on the transverse surface. r = ray.

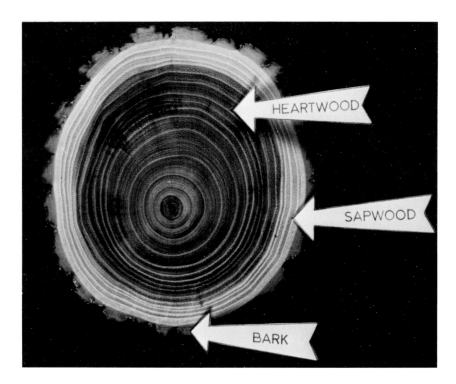

Figure 6. Heartwood and sapwood in a hardwood species exhibiting darkly colored heartwood, black locust, *Robinia pseudoacacia*.

Sapwood-Heartwood

If an entire cross-section of a tree can be examined, it is quite rare not to be able to see a difference in the color of the wood in the outer shell as contrasted with the inner core of the stem (Figure 6). Most species have a darker heartwood, the older tissue that was produced twenty, fifty, or even several hundred years before the tree was felled. The lighter-colored sapwood may be present as a rather wide band in young trees or a very narrow barely distinguishable ring in very old or large trees.

Certain species exhibit very little difference between sapwood and heartwood. Often this is because the heartwood is not rich in extractives, which are usually dark in color. The true boundary between the two regions is not the color line, although it often coincides with it, but the point at which the long-lived parenchyma cells of the wood rays finally die. By definition, heartwood contains no living ray or longitudinal parenchyma cells. The deposition by diffusion of the colored extractives is a phenomenon that accompanies this senescence and produces a pattern that approximates the sapwood-heartwood boundary.

Wood Rays

If viewed on an exact radial plane, wood rays appear as ribbons of tissue extending from the point of origin to the bark (Figures 4, 7, 18). In some species the rays are only a few cells high (along the axis of the tree stem), while in others such as the oaks, some of the wood rays are distinctive broad bands many cells in height. A variety of sizes may be found in a single species, while in other woods the rays may be uniform in size and spacing. Since rays are initiated by the cambium as needed, it follows that ray length is indeterminate.

The width of a wood ray can be observed in two planes, the cross-section and the tangential section. Very narrow rays may be uniseriate (one cell wide) and some wide rays may be aggregates (a composite of small rays and fibers or vessels that appears like a wide ray) very readily observed even without a hand lens. On the tangential section it is possible to see both width and height of rays, and the distribution or spacing, any of which might contribute to a distinctive pattern that can be related to a species or group of species.

Texture and Grain

These terms are used interchangeably and ambiguously by many persons who work with wood. Generally, texture describes the sizes (diameters) of the important cells in wood and to some extent the sizes of the tissues (rays, etc.). Grain refers to the general direction of the major longitudinal fibers of wood in relation to the axis of the tree stem or to the plane of the sawn or cut surfaces or edges.

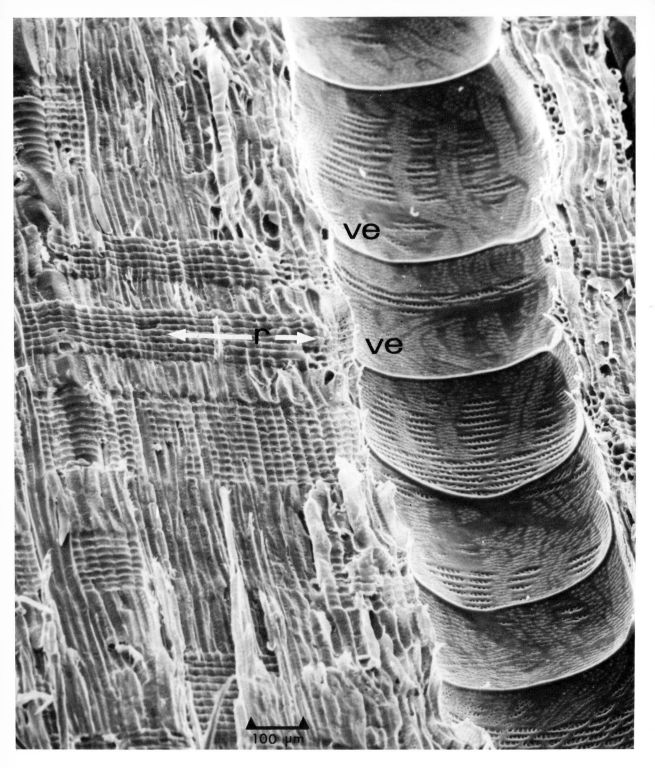

Figure 7. Scanning electron micrograph of the radial surface of a hardwood, red oak, *Quercus* sp., showing wood rays (r) and the heavily pitted walls of vessel elements (ve). Pit types vary with the nature of the cell in contact with the vessel.

Examples are spiral grain for simple deviation and blister, curly, and birdseye grain for complex variations. Grain distortions result in distinctive figure and may enhance the value of wood for decorative purposes.

Color

Color is one of the most conspicuous characteristics of wood and, although quite variable, is one of the important features used in identification as well as adding aesthetic value. Usually only the heartwood has distinctive color. Different shades of color may be present in various samples of wood, and these shades are difficult to describe. Experience and sample comparison are important when using color in identification. Heartwood colors range from cream to black, with shades of brown and reddish brown being very common.

Odor and Taste

Certain woods have distinctive odors, while a very few have distinctive tastes. Odors are rather difficult to describe so memory and comparison are very helpful. Scented woods range from spicy or cedar-like to unpleasant in odor. Sassafras among the hardwoods and the "cedars" of the softwoods are well known for their aromatic character. There are numerous tropical woods with characteristic odors.

Weight, Moisture Content, and Specific Gravity

Of all the characteristics of wood, weight and specific gravity are near the top of the list for difficulty in understanding by the beginner. The problem derives from two wood properties. The first is that wood is hygroscopic. It picks up or loses moisture as the surroundings change in temperature and relative humidity. The second is that wood shrinks or swells in volume as it loses or gains water within certain limits. When a piece of wood is weighed, the moisture present is included and some knowledge of its moisture content is necessary. Moisture content from 5 to 25 percent may be determined using various moisture meters developed for this purpose. The most accurate method in all cases is to follow the laboratory procedure of weighing the piece with moisture, removing the moisture by drying in an oven (105° C.), and reweighing. The equation for determining moisture content is:

$$\text{M.C. \%} = \frac{\text{weight of wood with water} - \text{oven dry weight}}{\text{oven dry weight}} \times 100$$

Specific gravity is even more difficult for the beginner to comprehend. Specific gravity is defined as the weight of a substance compared to the weight of an equivalent volume of water. However, both the weight of the wood and its volume change with changes in moisture content. For valid comparisons, the values used must be specified. The weight that is easiest to obtain is the oven dry weight, while the green volume requires the least preparation.

The value obtained is called the basic specific gravity (b.s.p.) and the equation becomes:

$$\text{b.s.p.} = \frac{\text{oven dry weight of sample}}{\text{weight of displaced volume of water}}$$
(when sample is green or at maximum volume)

Wood reaches its maximum volume when the moisture content is above the fiber-saturation point. This is approximately 30 percent. The term "green" refers to the unseasoned condition of wood and may range as high as 200 percent moisture content in native woods. The volume would be no greater than at the fiber-saturation point.

For the commercial woods covered in this manual, the basic specific gravity ranges approximately from 0.29 to 0.81. Arbitrary classifications may be established within this range so that woods can be categorized as light, moderately heavy, or heavy. It may be of interest that both lighter and heavier woods than indicated by the range above can be found, both as native species and imported tropical woods.

Hardness

This property, like many strength properties, is closely related to specific gravity. In a given sample it will change as moisture content varies. However, since the specific gravity of wood may range from .10 to 1.10, so too may hardness. A crude method of determining hardness of wood is the fingernail test. A "soft" wood may be indented by this method, while a "hard" wood will not be so readily damaged. As for other materials, there is a standard test and specifications for the determination of hardness using testing machines.

MICROSCOPIC STRUCTURE OF WOOD

The basic building unit of wood is the cell. A piece of lumber is composed of vast numbers of these elements, all held together as a natural composite material by an intercellular substance rich in lignin. The chemical removal of this cementing material is called pulping and is the basis for the papermaking industry which utilizes wood fiber.

A cut made on the cross-section of a block of wood using a sharp pocket knife or a razor blade will help reveal the cellular composition of this unique material, provided a hand lens is used. The resolving power of the unaided eye is inadequate to image these cells which may be as small as 25 micrometers (μm) in diameter (approximately 1/1000th of an inch). As will be noted in Chapter 2, "Features Useful for Wood Identification," diagnostic studies based on gross and hand lens features will often be sufficient to identify many species, especially those having unusual characteristics. However, there are groups of woods which cannot be readily identified without the aid of a light microscope. Perhaps it should be mentioned that in some instances even this evidence is inadequate.

The light microscope generally does provide the necessary evidence for identification. To use this tool effectively requires some basic skill in specimen preparation and microscope operation. The fundamentals have been outlined in the appendices of this manual. Additionally, the general characteristics of wood structure as viewed with the light microscope must be familiar before the specific diagnostic features can be of much use.

Wood Cells

All cells in wood may be divided into two broad categories: parenchyma and prosenchyma. Parenchyma cells retain their protoplasm for many years after formation at the cambium. Wood rays are composed essentially of ray parenchyma cells and sometimes, in a few conifers, with limited numbers of prosenchyma cells. There are also longitudinal parenchyma cells distributed in patterns that may be helpful in wood identification. Some parenchyma cells assume specialized functions, but most of them serve as food storage reservoirs and provide communciation channels radially from the cambium into the sapwood. Of course the latter function is limited to ray parenchyma cells.

Prosenchyma cells lose their contents within a short time after formation in the cambial zone. After differentiation into various specialized forms, and creation of a thickened wall, the cytoplasmic material is largely eluted and recycled by the tree. Sap conduction is an essential function of prosenchymatous elements such as vessels, tracheids, and other large-lumened cells, although this may be limited to a single growing season. Mechanical support is a function that continues for the life of the tree since the wood cell (without its living contents) is essentially the skeletal framework of the tree stem.

Cell Types

To grasp the concept of cell arrangement as it relates to species characteristics there is considerable advantage in first seeing the separated individual cells. Maceration, which is actually pulping on a small scale, frees the cells one from another and then their shape, size, surface structure, and other details can be examined using the microscope.

In Figure 8 cells from both softwoods and hardwoods are illustrated at equivalent magnification so that comparison of size and shape can be readily made. It may not be easy to imagine the role of these individual cells in the composite material, wood. Yet, if the softwood tracheid (Figure 8e) were examined in cross-section, its shape would suggest that it fits into a more ordered arrangement than the vessel segments (Figures 8a, 8b, 8c) or the libriform fiber (Figure 8d) from hardwoods. Softwoods do appear to be of simpler structure, with tracheids arranged in radial rows and representing the only major type of longitudinal element. Hardwoods have many types of longitudinal elements and there is generally far less radial arrangement than in coniferous woods. Axial (strand) parenchyma may be absent, sparse, or abundant in both hardwoods and softwoods. The occurrence, arrangement, and, to some extent, the sculpturing may be of diagnostic value. Cell size and cell shape as well as pattern of cell distribution are characteristic for each hardwood species.

The tracheid in conifers is a long cell (average 3.5 to 5 mm.) with rounded or tapered ends. In earlywood tracheids the cell cavity or lumen is larger, but in latewood tracheids it is much narrower. As tracheids provide both conduction and mechanical support there is less specialization of structure than in hardwood elements. The walls are marked by bordered pits which provide pathways for conduction of fluids to adjoining tracheids (Figure 9).

Other cell types in softwoods include ray parenchyma, a short, brick-shaped cell oriented horizontally in the wood ray. The ray often incorporates ray tracheids, generally at its upper and lower margins; these are prosenchymatous cells, often irregularly shaped and having bordered pits in contrast with the simple pitting found in the ray parenchyma.

A special parenchyma cell is found surrounding resin cavities in conifers. This type of cell is the source of resin which is secreted into the cavity. This combination of epithelial cells surrounding a cavity is called a resin canal. Longitudinal resin canals may be observed on the transverse

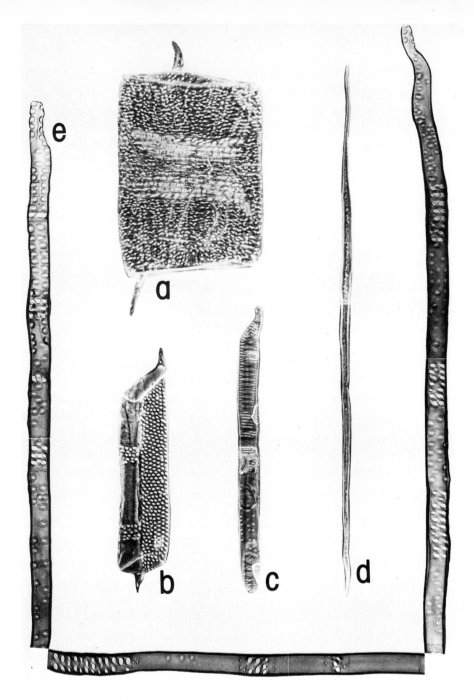

Figure 8. Photomicrographs of some hardwood and softwood cell types illustrating the comparative size and shape of various elements. Note especially how much longer the coniferous tracheid (e) is than the vessel segments (a, b, and c). A libriform fiber is shown at (d). To give an indication of scale, the softwood tracheid is approximately 3.5 mm. in length.

surface and horizontal resin canals are found incorporated into so-called fusiform rays of the conifers in which they occur. Figures 3, 4, and 40 include examples of normal resin canals.

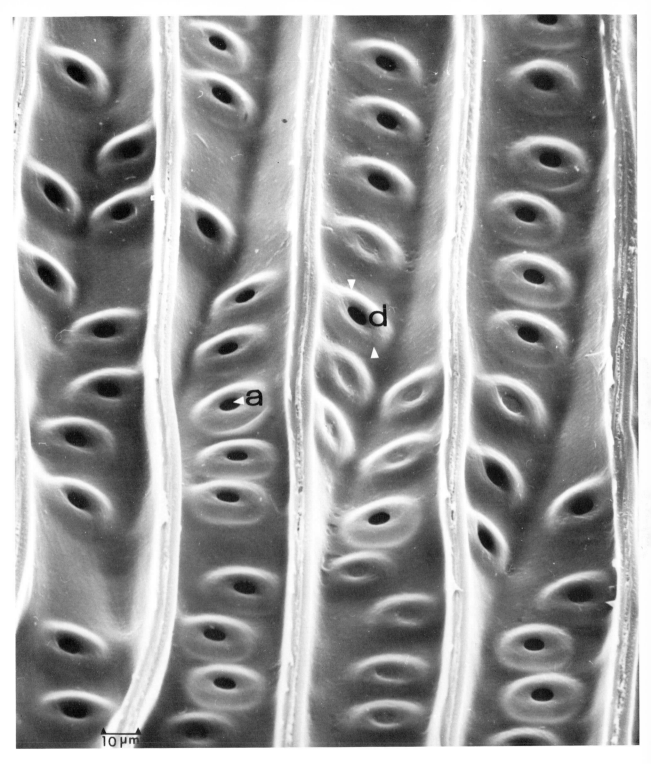

Figure 9. Scanning electron micrograph of coniferous tracheids in eastern white pine, *Pinus strobus*, showing bordered pits on the radial walls. Note how the bordered pit dome (d) projects into the cell lumen. The pit aperture (a) provides access to the pit chamber, and ultimately fluid can flow to the adjoining tracheid if the pit pair is not aspirated.

Vessels are not found in softwoods, but they occur invariably in all native hardwoods. The vessel is an articulated structure composed of an indeterminate number of vessel elements, a cell type that has openings or perforations at either end and is aligned vertically with other elements to form a continuous channel. There are many micrographs illustrating vessel structure in this manual including Figures 5, 7, 9, 16a–c, 19, and 31a. As mentioned previously, the cross-section of a vessel is known as a pore.

Vessel elements have many shapes and sizes varying with species and location within a growth increment. Figure 9 was designed to illustrate some of this variation found in vessels as well as to compare vessels with conifer tracheids and libriform fibers from hardwoods. Additional cell types found in native woods are given in Table 3 with a notation indicating which elements are always present in every species in each of the two major categories of woods.

SUBMICROSCOPIC STRUCTURE OF WOOD

Wood is a natural composite material and a chemical complex of cellulose, lignin, hemicelluloses, and extractives. The framework substance is cellulose, which occurs in the form of microfibrils, long strands which make up from 40 to 50 percent of the wood. Hemicelluloses are the matrix materials that fill the voids around the microfibrils. Finally, the system is incrusted with lignin that can be found throughout the cell wall and in the intercellular region where its packing density is very high. The lignin content of wood ranges from 18 to 25 percent in hardwoods and 25 to 35 percent in softwoods. Softwoods consist of about 20 percent hemicellulose, while hardwoods average around 30 percent. Extractives and inorganic constituents total from 2 to 30 percent of the wood volume.

Table 3

CELL TYPES OF HARDWOODS AND SOFTWOODS

Hardwoods	Softwoods

LONGITUDINAL ELEMENTS OF PROSENCHYMA

Hardwoods	Softwoods
*Vessel elements	*Tracheids
*Fiber tracheids	Resinous tracheids
and/or	
*Libriform fibers	Strand tracheids
Vascular tracheids	
Vasicentric tracheids	

LONGITUDINAL ELEMENTS OF PARENCHYMA

Hardwoods	Softwoods
Strand parenchyma	Strand parenchyma
Fusiform parenchyma	
Epithelial parenchyma	Epithelial parenchyma

HORIZONTAL ELEMENTS OF PROSENCHYMA

Hardwoods	Softwoods
None	Ray tracheids

HORIZONTAL ELEMENTS OF PARENCHYMA

Hardwoods	Softwoods
*Ray parenchyma	*Ray parenchyma
Upright cells	
Procumbent cells	
Epithelial parenchyma	Epithelial parenchyma

*These elements invariably are present in native woods. Others may occur as characteristic of certain woods.

Cell Wall Organization

In normal cell walls of both softwoods and hardwoods, the cellulose microfibrils are aggregated into thin lamellae which are, in turn, organized into layers. The walls usually contain three layers of secondary origin, that is, the portion of the cell wall that was produced by the living protoplasm of the cell. The outer envelope of the cell is termed "primary wall" and consists of a loose network of microfibrils with other materials as well. This primary wall exists at the time the cell is formed in the cambium.

The secondary wall layers are designated as S1, S2, and S3, from the outside to the inner layer lining the cell lumen. Within each layer the microfibrils are oriented more or less uniformly into a rather dense parallel array. The S1 has its microfibrils oriented predominantly almost perpendicular to the long axis of the cell. The S2 is the principal layer of the wall. It is generally thicker than either the S1 or the S3 and since it is oriented approximately parallel to the cell axis, it contributes most to the mechanical properties of the cell. Finally, the S3 is a thin layer having its orientation parallel that of the S1. In essence then, there is a natural three-ply construction within the normal cell wall (Figure 10). This structure provides stiffness and other characteristics that make the wood cell unique for its size and related physical behavior.

Some species of wood will exhibit an additional layer over the S3 in the form of a rough or warty surface. This so-called warty layer is typical of the hard pines, some cedars, and other softwoods. Warts are also found in hardwoods such as beech. It was first hoped that this very fine structure would provide additional evidence for the separation of species that are difficult to identify. However, the warty layer is too variable to be of substantial diagnostic value. In any case, an electron microscope would be needed in analyzing this feature because the warts are generally beyond the resolving power of the light microscope.

In the electron micrographs (Figures 11 and 12) the microfibrillar nature of the cell wall and the relatively coarse nature of the warty layer are clearly demonstrated. The hemicellulose and lignin are present, but their amorphous nature makes their detection by this means difficult. It is possible to

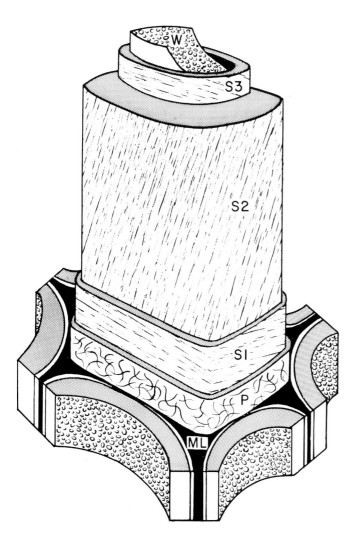

Figure 10. Diagram summarizing the structural evidence now available to characterize the organization of the wood cell wall. P = primary wall; ML = middle lamella or intercellular layer; S1, S2, and S3 refer to the outer, middle, and inner layers of the secondary wall, respectively; W = warty layer. From *Wood Ultrastructure—An Atlas of Electron Micrographs*, *by Wilfred A. Côté, Jr.*, by permission of University of Washington Press, publisher.

remove all of the carbohydrate materials chemically, thus leaving a lignin skeleton which can be viewed in the electron microscope (Figure 13).

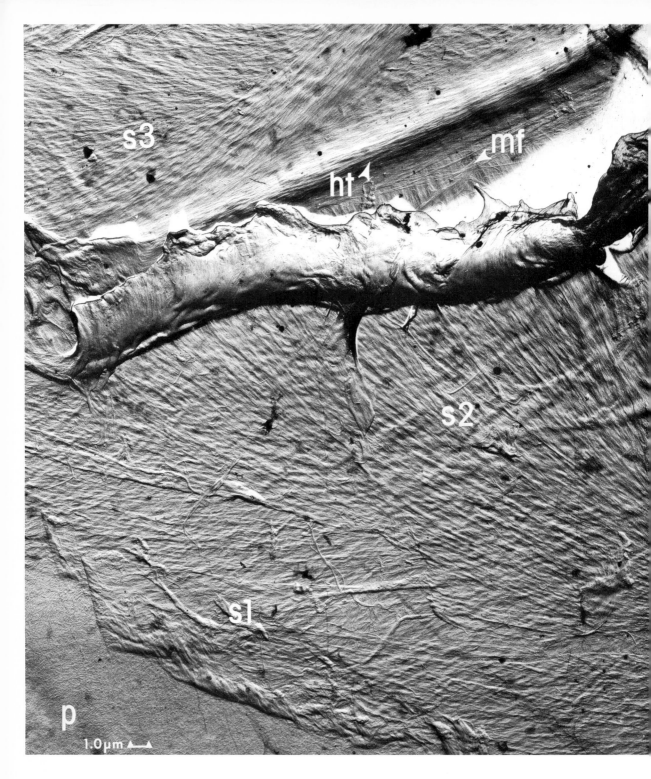

Figure 11. Transmission electron micrograph of the wood cell wall showing cellulose microfibrils (mf) and their organization into layers of varying orientation: p = primary wall; S1, S2, and S3 layers of the secondary wall. The helical thickenings (ht) are found in only a few species of softwood such as this Douglas-fir, *Pseudotsuga menziesii*, and form part of the S3 layer. Replica technique, cut surface. From *Wood Ultrastructure—An Atlas of Electron Micrographs*, by Wilfred A. Côté, Jr., by permission of University of Washington Press, publisher.

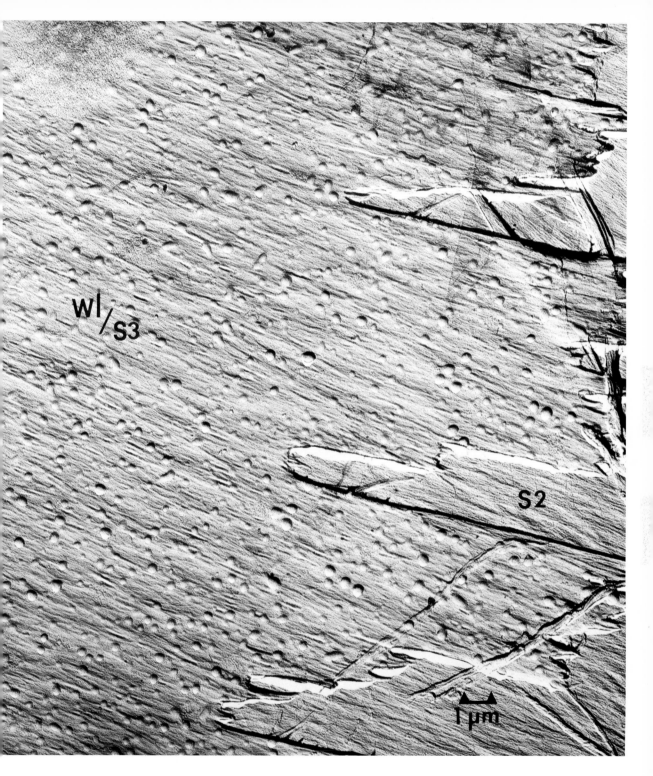

Figure 12. Transmission electron micrograph of the lumen lining of a tracheid of a southern yellow pine, *Pinus rigida*, pitch pine, revealing the nature of the warty layer (wl) which is superimposed over the S3 or inner layer of the secondary cell wall. The microfibrillar orientation of the S3 remains visible under the warty layer in this instance, but in some cases the microfibrils are completely masked. At the right both the S3 and the warty layer have been ruptured in specimen preparation and the S2 layer is visible.

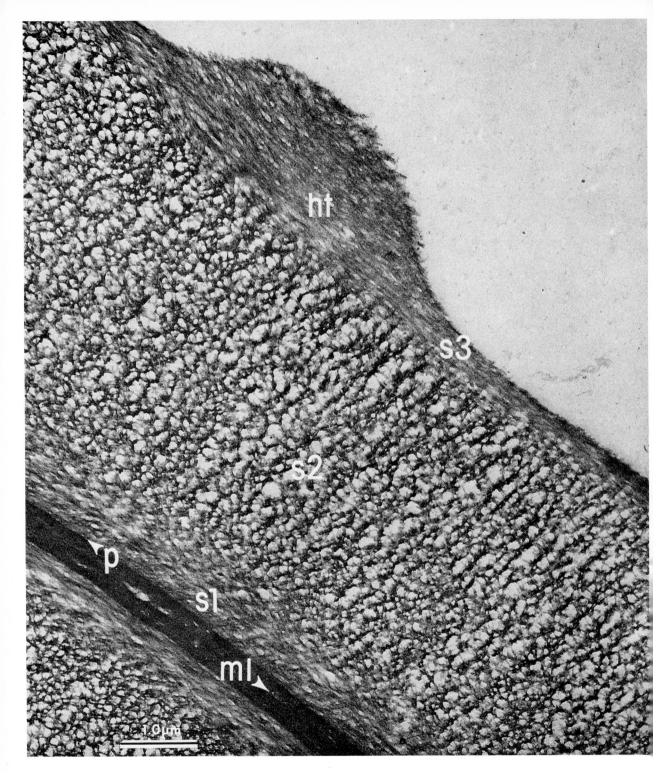

Figure 13. Transmission electron micrograph of an ultra-thin section through a ''lignin skeleton'' of a Douglas-fir tracheid illustrating the existence of fine pores where cellulose microfibrils were removed chemically. Note the retention of orientation distinct for each of the three secondary cell wall layers: S1, S2, and S3. The primary wall (p) and the middle lamella (ml) can also be identified. Note how the helical thickening (ht) forms part of the S3 layer.

Although most native woods have three-layered secondary walls, there are conditions under which both hardwoods and softwoods produce cells having fewer or more layers. This is reaction wood. Figures 14a and 14b provide examples of this abnormal wood.

Reaction Wood

Although reaction wood is abnormal, it occurs frequently enough that one should learn to recognize structural features that will make its identification relatively simple. This is stressed for the additional reason that the properties of reaction wood make it undesirable for some applications, and it should be eliminated from certain critical uses.

Both compression wood (softwoods) and tension wood (hardwoods) are produced in leaning trees, the former on the lower or underside of a stem and the latter on the upper side. The characteristic cell types are located in an eccentric portion of the tree trunk. That is, in the growth increments involved, the compression wood portion is much wider than the normal wood. The same applies to tension wood in hardwoods, but it must be stressed that the eccentricities occur on the upper side in broad-leaved species and the underside in softwoods. Similarities between compression wood and tension wood end there.

The wood in the compression wood rings of a softwood have a reddish, "dead" appearance. A thin section held over a light source shows the compression wood as an opaque zone contrasted with the translucent normal wood. Compression wood is weaker under impact loading and is therefore unsuitable for many uses. Figure 14a shows how different the cell walls of compression wood tracheids are from normal cells. They lack an S3 layer and have large voids in the S2. A light microscope view (Figure 50a) shows these voids as spiral checks while in cross-section compression wood is seen to have rounded tracheids and intercellular spaces. In addition to these easily recognized structural deviations from the normal, the chemical composition of compression wood is different. There is more lignin and less cellulose in the cell walls. This explains, in part at least, why

Figure 14a. Scanning electron micrograph of compression wood, the reaction wood of conifers. Note the absence of an S3 layer and the presence of large voids or gaps within the S2 layer of the cell wall. The rounded configuration of the cells as viewed in cross-section, and the intercellular spaces are typical of this abnormal wood. Douglas-fir, *Pseudotsuga menziesii.*

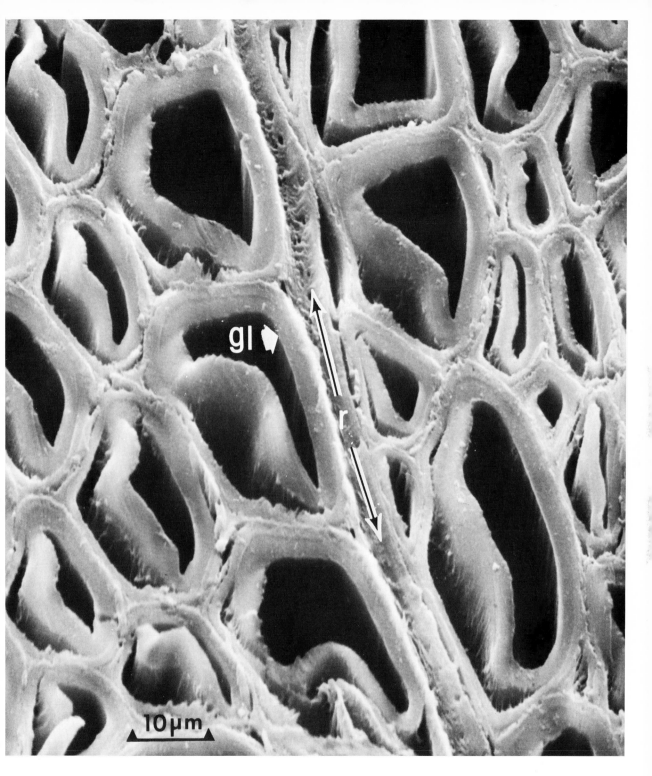

Figure 14b. Scanning electron micrograph of tension wood, the reaction wood of hardwoods. Note the loose, inner "gelatinous" layer (gl) lining the cell lumen. This layer is unlignified and its presence char- acterizes the so-called tension fibers. A ray (r) tra- verses the cross-section of this specimen of poplar, *Populus* sp.

compression wood may be weaker than normal wood. Cellulose contributes most to the strength properties of wood, especially tensile strength.

Tension wood is found frequently, but its importance is less than that of compression wood. Hardwoods are not utilized to the same extent for structural applications. In this abnormality, fibers which would be expected to have a three-layered secondary wall may have fewer or more than three. The feature that characterizes tension wood is the so-called gelatinous layer (G-layer), which is illustrated very clearly in Figure 14b. This is a cellulosic layer that is unlignified. Thus it appears in the light microscope as a gelatinous or soft layer. Although it is a misnomer, "gelatinous layer" is difficult to change in the literature or in everyday use. The correct term for a cell with such a layer is "tension wood fiber." The G-layer may be present when there is only an S1, or it may be found when both an S1 and an S2 are present. Occasionally an S3 is also in the cell wall so that the G-layer is, in a sense, an extra layer.

In many instances the G-layer appears to be separated from the remainder of the cell wall, although it might have been pulled loose in cutting. Undoubtedly it is loosely attached.

The surface of a piece of hardwood lumber containing tension wood fibers will exhibit a woolly or fuzzy appearance. This is the result of the tension wood fibers' pulling loose rather than cutting cleanly. For furniture manufacturing and other uses, this is an obvious defect.

Cell Wall Sculpturing

Although most cells are constructed of microfibrillar layers in the S1, S2, and S3 configuration described and illustrated earlier, it should be apparent from many of the illustrations in this manual that the cell walls are interrupted or sculptured in a number of ways. The warty layer masks the structure of the underlying S3 in the example shown in Figure 11. However, this type of sculpturing is not found in all species or in all cells of a given species. Where it does occur, as in this representative of the southern yellow pines, it can be extremely variable in thickness, in wart size, and in distribution. Therefore the warty layer is of somewhat limited diagnostic value.

Helical Thickening

Another form of sculpturing is the helical thickening, also known as spiral thickening. One of these rope-like structures appears near the top of the electron micrograph in Figure 10. Its microfibrillar organization in this example from Douglas-fir is quite apparent and can be further interpreted from the "lignin skeleton" in Figure 13. Helical thickenings are part of the S3 layer of the secondary wall. A three-dimensional view of a number of Douglas-fir tracheids exhibiting this cell wall modification is included as Figure 55. Among the softwoods, Pacific yew and Douglas-fir have such sculptured cell walls. In the hardwoods, one can find helical thickenings in vessels of basswood (Figures 28a and 31a) and in various kinds of cells or portions of cells, in other species. Table 7 summarizes this distribution.

Pitting

The most common sculpturing of the cell walls in wood is due to pitting. Pits are gaps or interruptions in the secondary wall. They extend from the cell cavity or lumen to the original cell envelope, the primary wall, which forms the outer or closing membrane. A pit may appear as a depression in the wall or may form a canal or channel from lumen to membrane, depending on cell wall thickness. If it occurs in a parenchyma cell wall there is generally no overhanging border and it is termed a "simple pit." In a cell of the prosenchyma type such as a coniferous tracheid or a hardwood vessel, there is usually a pit chamber with a border enclosing it except at the aperture. This type of pit is known as a "bordered pit." The cell wall sculpturing that is typical of a bordered pit in a softwood tracheid is illustrated in Figure 8 which shows a dome projecting from the radial tracheid wall into the cell lumen. The aperture in the center of the dome provides access to the chamber and to the membrane suspended within it. A disk in the center of the membrane may move to either aperture of a bordered pit pair, in the case of coniferous woods, but not in hardwoods.

Fluid flow from one cell to another is possible because pits generally occur in pairs; that is, a pit in one cell matches exactly one in an adjacent cell wall. In describing wood anatomy, pits are often referred to as pit pairs. If two simple pits are joined, the result is a "simple pit pair." A "bordered pit pair" consists of two bordered pits and the combined pit membranes at the junction of the primary walls. When a parenchyma cell, such as in a ray, is joined to a longitudinal tracheid (the usual combination in cross-field pitting in softwoods), the pit pairs are termed "half-bordered."

Figures 14c through 14f are electron micrographs which provide graphic evidence for the structure of pits and pit pairs in conifers. The figure captions describe the anatomical features of pits in greater detail. Pit structure in hardwoods is similar as far as terminology is concerned. Simple pits have a membrane of primary wall with no visible openings at electron microscope levels of magnification, for the most part. The main difference between hardwood and softwood pitting is found in the bordered pit pairs. As may be seen in the micrographs, especially Figure 14f, a torus is often present in the center of a porous membrane in conifers. Pit aspiration or sealing is therefore a possibility. In the hardwood bordered pit pairs there is no torus and the membrane is similar to that of the simple pits. Fluid movement is assumed to be mostly by diffusion across the membrane.

Further discussion about pits will be found at appropriate points in the manual where identification may be based on particular pit features.

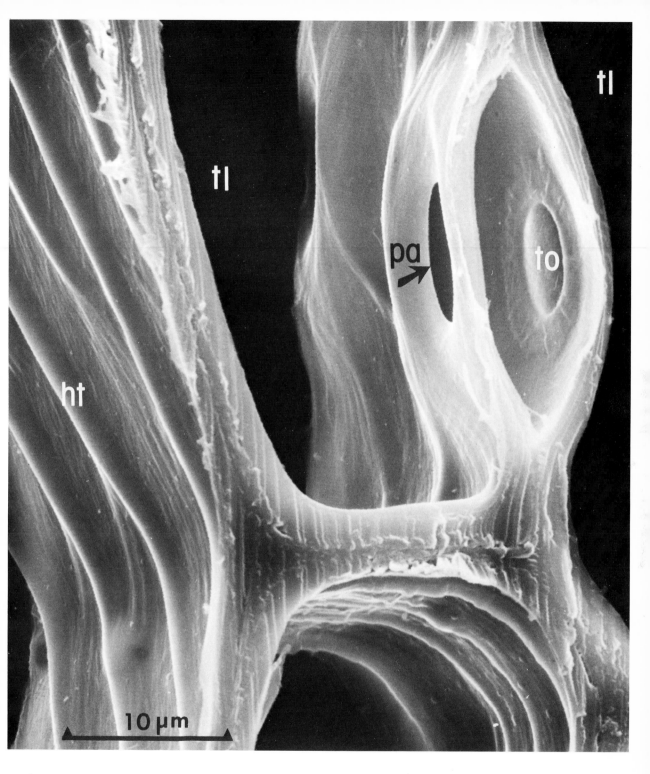

Figure 14c. Scanning electron micrograph of a cross-section of Douglas-fir wood affording a view into the lumens of four tracheids (tl) and a sectional view of a bordered pit pair joining two tracheids. Helical thickenings (ht) line the cell cavities. At the upper right the pit torus (to) is sealed against the pit aperture leading into the tracheid at extreme right. Note that the other pit aperture (pa) is open. This is typical for an aspirated bordered pit pair through which flow has been blocked effectively.

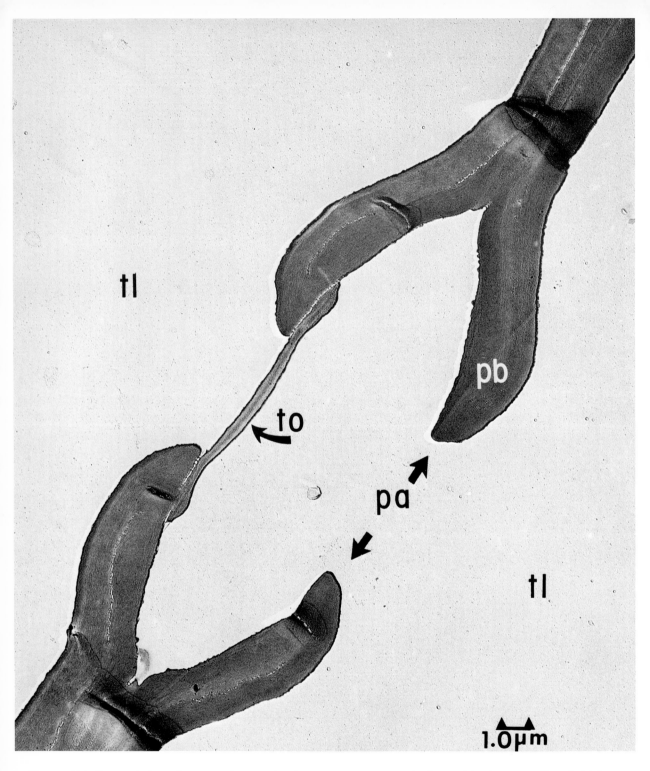

Figure 14d. Transmission electron micrograph of an ultra-thin section through a bordered pit pair in the wood of *Pinus echinata,* shortleaf pine, one of the southern yellow pines. This is an aspirated bordered pit pair with the torus (to) pressed against one pit aperture (pa) which would otherwise allow fluid flow between the two tracheids. Note that the pit borders (pb) project into the tracheid lumens (tl), forming a dome.

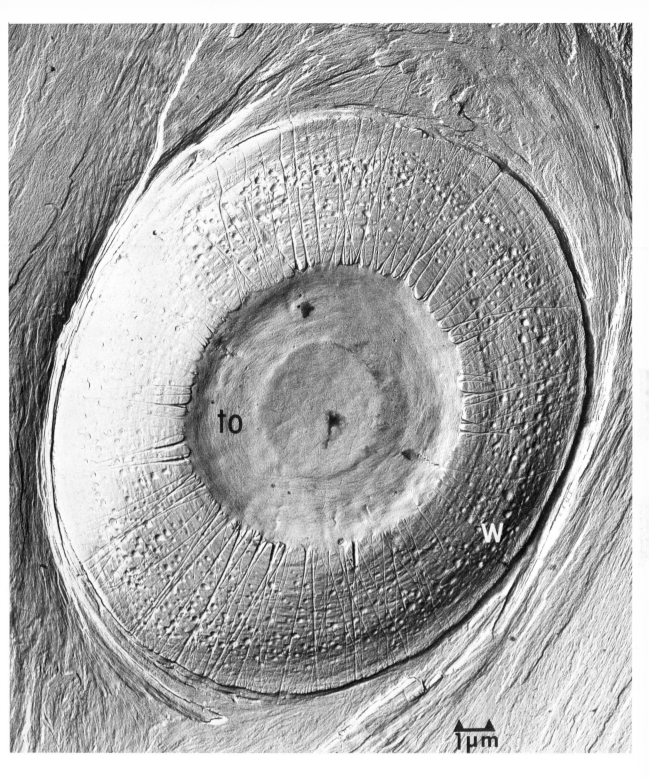

Figure 14e. Transmission electron micrograph of an aspirated bordered pit using the direct carbon replica technique. The torus (to), a central disk supported by fine cellulosic strands extending to the periphery of the pit chamber, has been drawn tightly into one of the two pit apertures in a pit pair, as can be seen in the dished center portion of the valve-like structure. Warts (w) line the pit chamber wall and are visible among the membrane strands. Virginia pine, *Pinus virginiana*, a southern yellow pine.

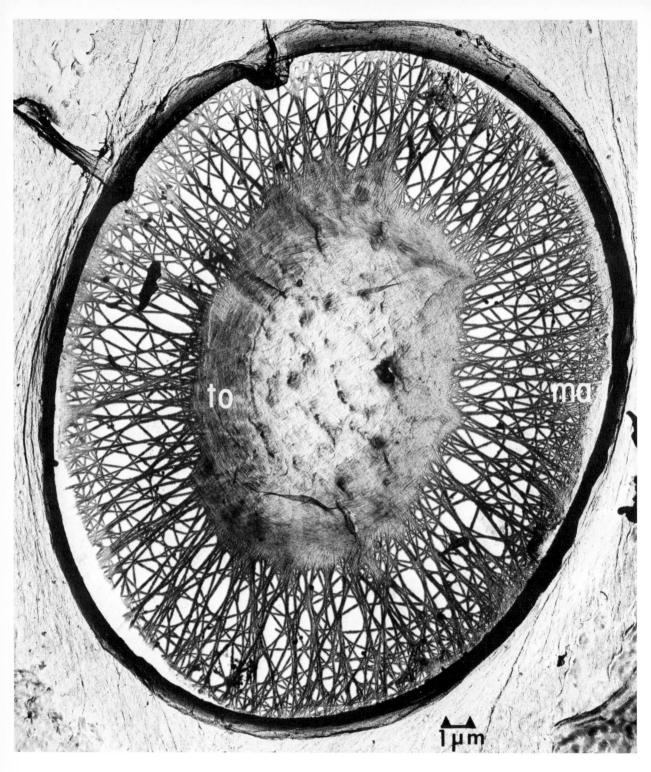

Figure 14f. Bordered pit in eastern white pine, *Pinus strobus*, prepared to minimize drying forces on the membrane and keeping it from aspirating. The supporting membrane (ma), also called the margo, is more clearly exhibited than in the previous micrograph because it is in the normal or median position within the pit chamber. The torus (to) is not sealing either aperture. Flow of fluids between two tracheids through such a membrane would be restricted only by the size of the openings. It should be noted that each tracheid has many such pits along its length. Transmission electron micrograph.

Features Useful for Wood Identification

INTRODUCTION

The process of identifying a piece of wood is a complex one even for the experienced wood anatomist. Although the various steps that one goes through may no longer be appreciated by such a specialist, in fact the procedure involves the integration of many bits of evidence. This subconscious procedure may begin with a quick overall inspection of the sample for color, figure, density, and other characteristics which may be assessed with the unaided eye.

The computer-like operation has perhaps already eliminated either the hardwoods or softwoods, certain genera, or even some species. The process then continues with an evaluation of odor or taste, if the nature of the sample suggests these, and then closer inspection of the sample surfaces for growth increment patterns, ray size, and distribution or other discernible evidence. The latter inspection often requires that the surface be cut cleanly to reveal detail. A sharp pocket knife or a razor blade are essential tools.

While many woods will have been identified by this point in the procedure, often it is necessary to consider macroscopic and microscopic features. These overlap to a considerable degree, depending on the vision and the skill or experience of the observer. A hand lens magnifies wood structure sufficiently to make the confirming identification in a large percentage of cases. However, it may be necessary to turn to a microscopic view for the separation of some of the softwoods, for example.

In the following pages, the macroscopic features have been separated from the microscopic, but the possibility of overlap of these areas should be kept in mind. Hand lens magnifications are a nominal 10X natural size, but in fact range from about 3X to 8X. If a light microscope is used, the lowest magnification possible is about 35X and may extend to 1200X, depending on the selection of optics used. The resolving power of any optical system is, of course, just as important as magnification. A discussion of some of these details may be found in the Appendices.

MACROSCOPIC FEATURES—HARDWOODS

The most important macroscopic features used in identifying hardwoods are considered in the following listing with detailed descriptions of their applicability and a variety of illustrations. Additional evidence appears in the section on microscopic features.

Ring- vs. Diffuse-Porous

Temperate zone hardwoods may be separated into two broad groups, ring-porous and diffuse-porous, on the basis of the change or lack of change of pore (vessel) size across the growth ring. A third separation, semi-ring-porous, also may be used but is rather variable. Ring-porous woods are those which show a distinct and rather sharp difference in the size of the pores in the earlywood portion of the growth ring compared with those of the latewood. The larger, earlywood pores may be in several rows or consist of a single, continuous, or interrupted row. Diffuse-porous woods have pores that appear the same regardless of position in the ring. Individual pores may vary but in random fashion. Semi-ring-porous woods show a gradual change in size across the ring. Figures 15 and 16 illustrate these structural features.

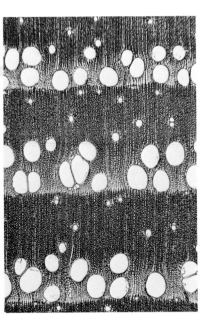 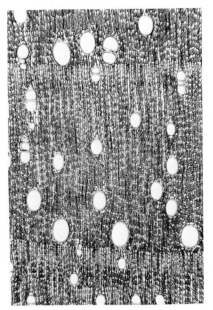 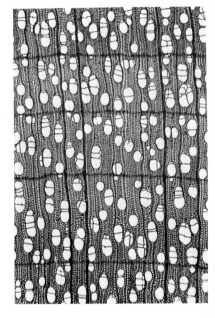

Ring-porous
Fraxinus nigra, 14X

Black ash

Other examples:
Quercus spp.
Carya spp.

Semi-ring-porous
Diospyros virginiana, 14X

Persimmon

Other examples:
Juglans spp.
Salix nigra

Diffuse-porous
Betula alleghaniensis, 14X

Yellow birch

Other examples:
Tilia americana
Acer spp.

Figure 15. Examples of hardwood groupings based on pore size change across the growth increment.

Genera falling within the groups defined above are given in Table 4. As noted in the table, a genus may appear in more than one group. This may be due to variation within a species as well as between species within a genus.

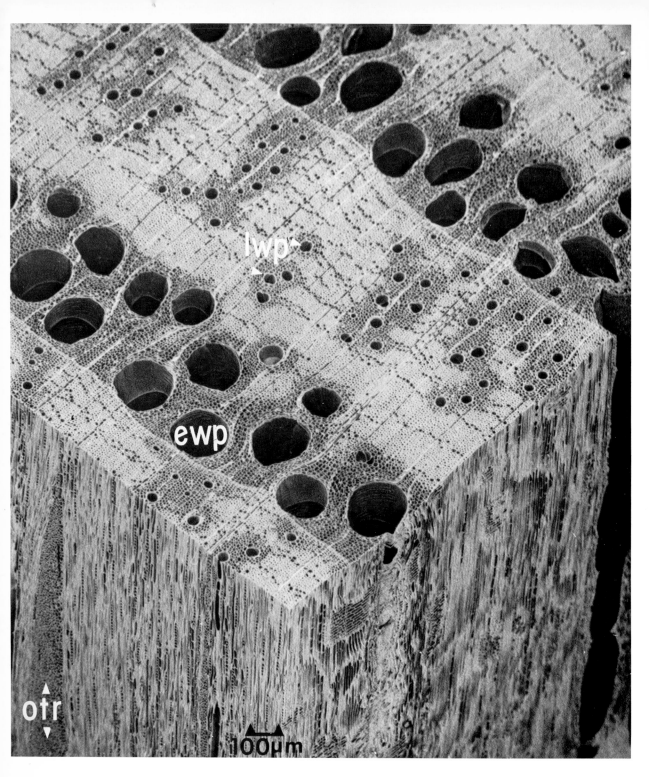

Figure 16a. Scanning electron micrograph of red oak, *Quercus rubra*, illustrating a ring-porous growth ring pattern. The springwood or earlywood pores (ewp) are large and concentrated in a narrow band at the beginning of the year's growth. Summerwood or late-wood pores (lwp) are much smaller. Note the broad oak-type ray (otr) on the tangential surface of the block.

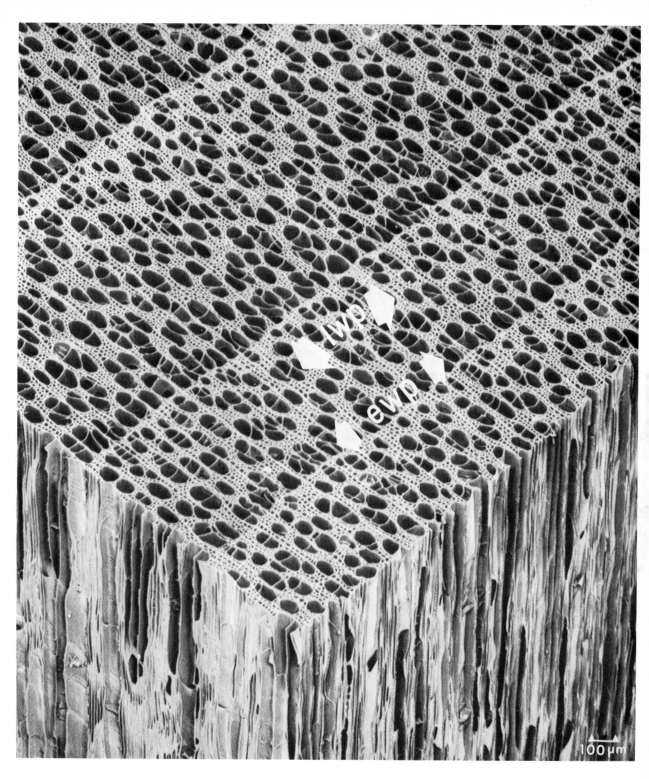

Figure 16b. Scanning electron micrograph of aspen, *Populus grandidentata,* illustrating a semi-ring-porous growth ring pattern in a hardwood. While the springwood or earlywood pores are larger and concentrated in a band at the beginning of the year's growth, the transition to smaller pores is more gradual than in a ring-porous pattern. ewp = earlywood pores; lwp = latewood pores.

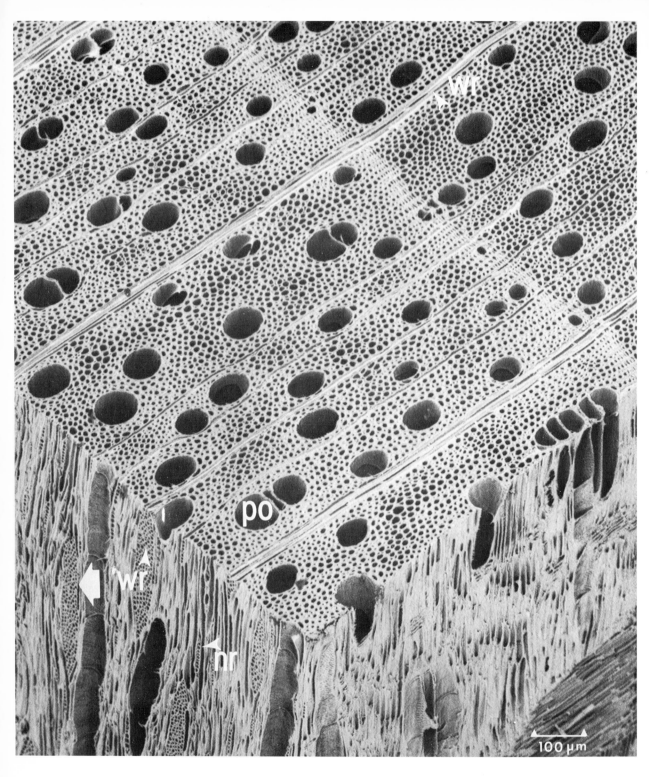

Figure 16c. In a diffuse-porous growth ring pattern, the vessels are more nearly uniform in size throughout the growth ring than in either ring-porous or semi-ring-porous patterns. The pores (po), or vessels viewed in cross-section, are generally distributed rather uniformly as well. This scanning electron micrograph of sugar maple, *Acer saccharum*, reveals that two sizes of rays are found in this species, the larger rays being as wide or wider than the pores. wr = wide ray; nr = narrow ray.

Table 4

Grouping of Hardwood Genera On the Basis of Growth Ring Change in Earlywood and Latewood		
Ring-Porous	Semi-Ring-Porous (Semi-Diffuse-Porous)	Diffuse-Porous
Carya	Carya	Acer
Castanea	Catalpa	Aesculus
Celtis	Diospyros	Alnus
Cercis	Juglans	Arbutus
Cladrastis	Lithocarpus	Betula
Fraxinus	Populus	Carpinus
Gleditsia	Prunus	Cercocarpus
Gymnocladus	Quercus	Cornus
Juglans	Rhamnus	Fagus
Maclura	Salix	Halesia
Morus		Ilex
Quercus		Liriodendron
Robinia		Magnolia
Sassafras		Nyssa
Ulmus		Ostrya
(Ailanthus)		Oxydendron
(Albizzia)		Persea
(Paulownia)		Platanus
		Populus
		Salix
		Tilia
		Umbellularia

(   ) = Naturalized species

Aggregate Rays

Large, relatively conspicuous rays are characteristic of *Quercus*, *Carpinus*, *Alnus* and *Lithocarpus*. In *Carpinus* and *Alnus*, the rays are aggregate structures composed of longitudinal and ray tissue rather than being strictly ray tissue. In *Carpinus* the aggregate rays are light in color and rather uniformly spaced. In *Alnus*, the wide rays are sporadically spaced, sometimes missing from individual pieces of wood. (See Figure 17.)

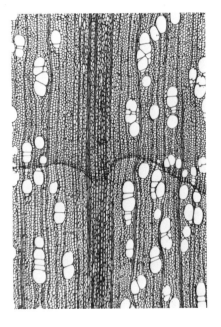 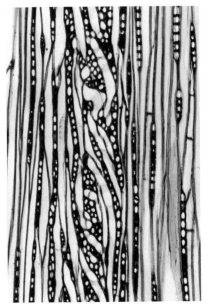

Carpinus caroliniana, 340X
American hornbeam
Other examples:
Alnus rubra
Lithocarpus spp.

Alnus rubra, 115X
Red alder
Other examples:
Lithocarpus spp.
Quercus spp. (occasionally)

Figure 17. Aggregate rays as may be seen on the cross-section and tangential surface of selected species.

Ray Size

Rays in the hardwoods vary from one cell in width to the larger tissues mentioned under Aggregate Rays. These may be as much as fifty cells in width. In certain woods, the rays are narrow and may not be visible to the unaided eye. In others, the rays will appear to be of two distinct sizes rather than intergrading from the smallest to the largest. Spacing of rays also is of some use, and the distinction usually is made as to whether they appear to occupy more or less than one-half of the transverse surface. For specifics regarding this feature, refer to Chapter 3 and to individual species descriptions in the bibliographies. (See Figure 18.)

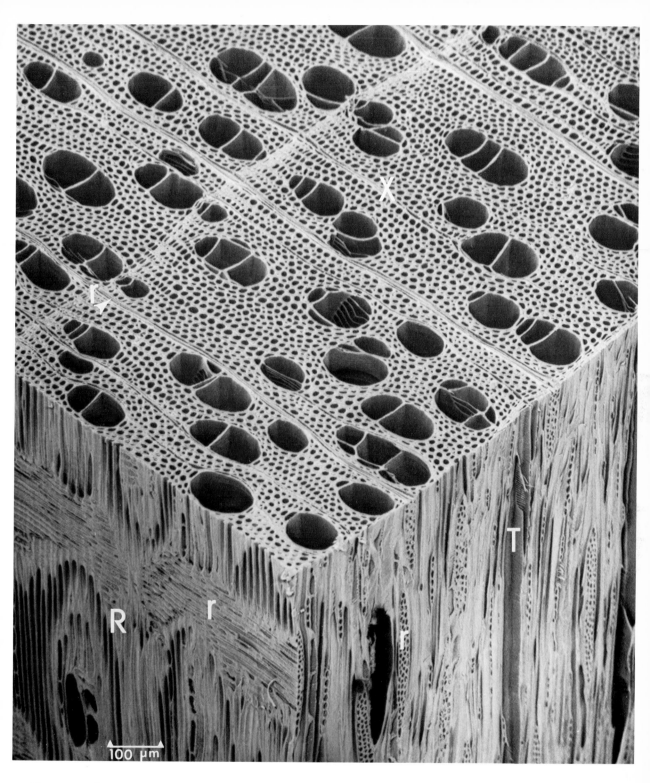

Figure 18. The size (width and height) of rays may be useful in identification of a wood species. In this scanning electron micrograph of yellow birch, *Betula alleghaniensis,* all three faces of a block, radial (R), tangential (T), and transverse (X), can be observed. The appearance of rays in each aspect and their relationship to other tissues can be readily appreciated. r = ray.

Storied Ray Structure

Storied structure of rays or longitudinal elements is more common in tropical woods than in the temperate zone hardwoods. Among native woods, persimmon and redbud, *Diospyros virginiana* and *Cercis canadensis*, respectively, invariably will show storied rays or ripple marks while *Aesculus* species will have storied rays most of the time. A few other woods will appear to have storied rays in part in individual samples. *Juglans* and *Fraxinus*, and rarely *Tilia* seem to be the most common. (See Figure 19.)

Pore Arrangement

In addition to showing up as ring-porous, diffuse-porous, or semi-ring-porous, pores may be distinctive in patterns of distribution in the latewood. The most common pattern is one of rather uniform distribution of pore multiples as may be seen in *Acer, Betula, Fagus,* and *Liriodendron*, as well as in many others. Pores essentially solitary is an unusual occurrence. Red gum, sourwood, and, to some extent, dogwood show this arrangement. Ulmiform pore arrangement is typical of the Ulmaceae (*Ulmus, Celtis*). Other woods also exhibit the ulmiform pattern in varying degrees. Among these are *Morus, Robinia, Maclura,* and *Cercis*. Dendritic pore arrangement is found in *Castanea, Quercus, Carpinus,* and *Ostrya. Ilex* exhibits radial lines of pore multiples called pore chains. *Alnus* also shows radial lines of pores to a limited extent. Nested pores are typical of *Gymnocladus, Ailanthus, Morus,* and *Maclura*. (See Figures 20a through 20f, and 21.)

Parenchyma Arrangement

While there are many variations and combinations of parenchyma arrangements, the following are most useful so far as viewing with a hand lens is concerned. Apotracheal banded parenchyma is an arrangement best illustrated in samples of *Carya* and *Diospyros*. This pattern can be seen in

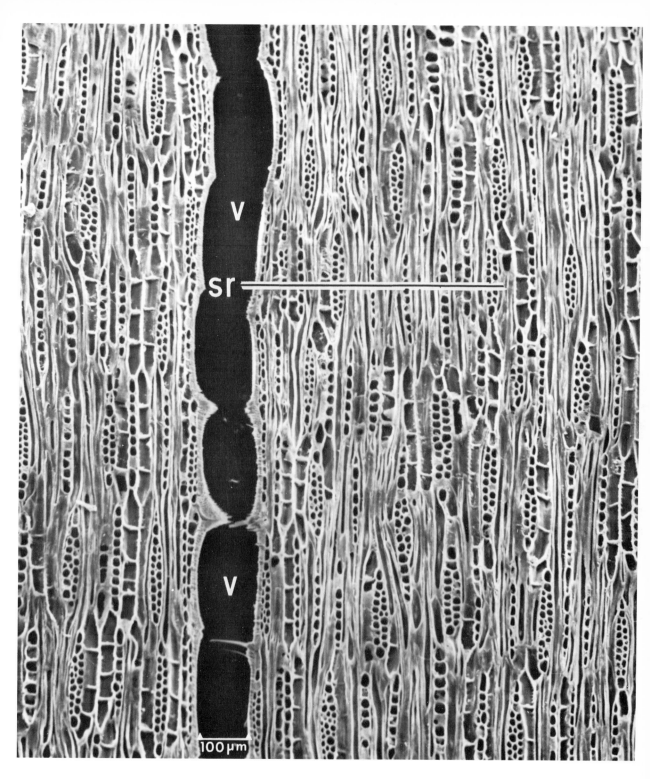

Figure 19. The arrangement of rays as viewed on the tangential surface is of diagnostic value. In some native woods, including the species represented here, persimmon, *Diospyros virginiana,* the rays are storied. When viewed with a hand lens or the unaided eye, this yields a pattern known as ripple marks that can be found on the tangential surface. It is a consistent feature of a few species and is found occasionally in a limited number of other species. Besides the storied rays (sr), one row of which has been highlighted with a bar through them, a vessel (v) is prominent in this scanning electron micrograph.

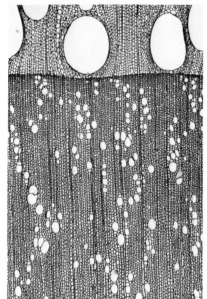

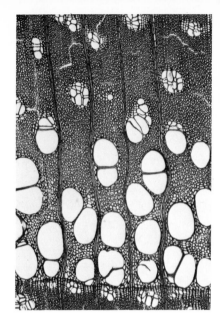

a. Ulmiform
Ulmus americana, 30X
American elm
Other examples:
Ulmus spp.
Celtis spp.

b. Dendritic
Castanea dentata, 30X
Chestnut
Other examples:
Ostrya spp.
Carpinus spp.

c. Nested
Gymnocladus dioicus, 30X
Kentucky coffeetree
Other examples:
Morus spp.
Ailanthus spp.
Robinia pseudoacacia

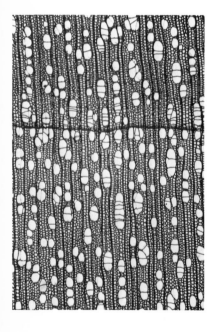

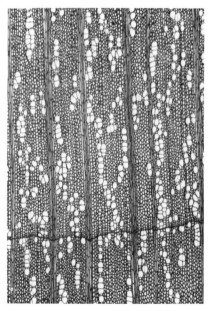

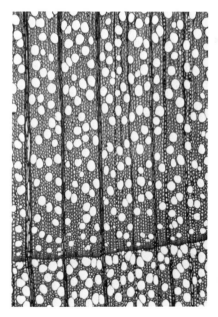

d. In multiples and radial lines
Alnus rubra, 30X
Red alder
Other examples:
Betula spp.
Acer spp.

e. In chains
Ilex opaca, 30X
American holly
Other example:
Carpinus caroliniana (in part)

f. Solitary (in part)
Oxydendron arboreum,
Sourwood
Other examples:
Liquidambar sp.
Cornus spp. (in part)

Figure 20. Pore (vessel) arrangement in various hardwoods.

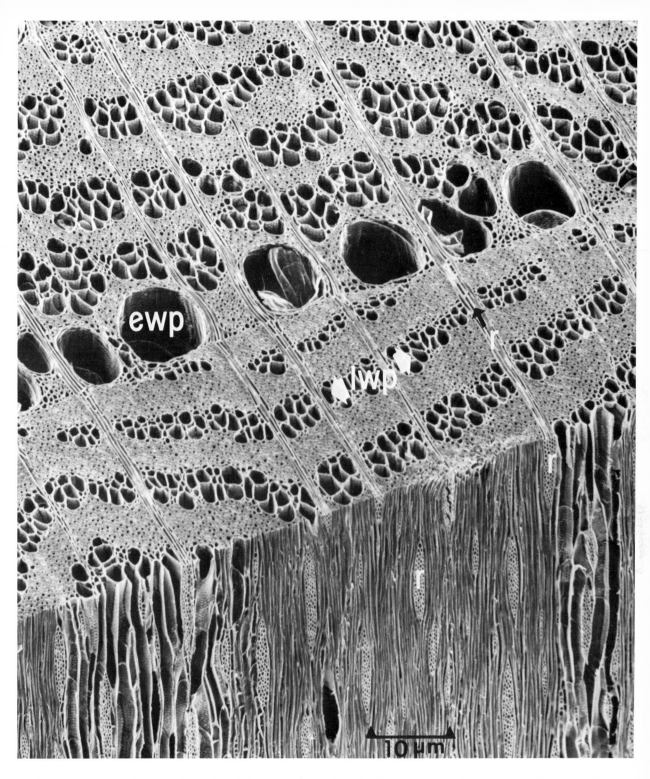

Figure 21. Some of the hardwoods exhibit characteristic pore patterns in addition to being ring-porous or diffuse-porous. Among them are the woods of the Ulmaceae *(Ulmus, Celtis)* represented by American elm, *Ulmus americana*, in this scanning electron micrograph. As can be seen, this is a ring-porous wood, but the latewood vessels are arranged in wavy lines that help make the identification of elms relatively easy. Precautions are suggested in the text because similar but less consistent patterns may be found in other hardwoods. ewp = earlywood pore; lwp = latewood pores; r = ray.

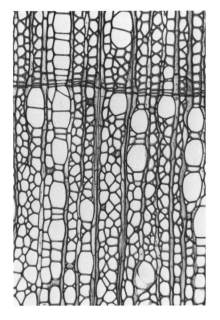 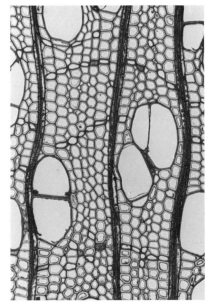

a. Apotracheal (diffuse)

Nyssa aquatica, 80X

Black gum

Other examples:
Liquidambar spp.
Platanus occidentalis

b. Apotracheal (diffuse in aggregates)

Betula papyrifera, 125X

Paper birch

Other examples:
Alnus rubra
Betula spp.

Figure 22. Examples of longitudinal (axial) parenchyma arrangement in hardwoods.

the latewood of *Fagus, Juglans, Carpinus, Ostrya,* and *Cornus* under optimum conditions. When visible, its presence is an aid in separating samples of *Cornus* from *Acer.* If definitely associated with the pores, this parenchyma arrangement may be called paratracheal banded.

Marginal parenchyma is found in a number of woods but is typical of *Liriodendron, Magnolia, Tilia, Salix, Populus,* and *Aesculus.* Usually it appears as a whitish line. In *Acer* the parenchyma is intermixed with fibers and appears as a brownish or dark line.

Paratracheal parenchyma is visible in a number of woods as a thick, light colored ring or zone around the pores or pore groups. *Fraxinus, Sassafras, Umbellularia,* and *Gleditsia* all show this arrangement to a noticeable degree. (See Figures 22a through 22h.)

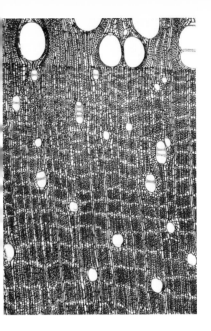

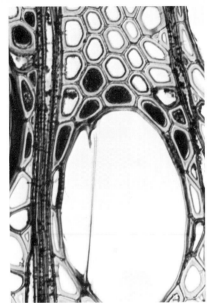

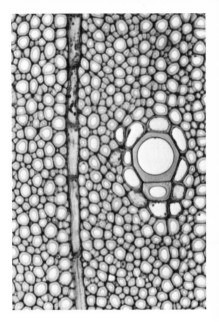

c. Apotracheal (banded)

Carya pecan, 30X

Pecan hickory

Other examples:
Tilia americana
Diospyros virginiana

d. Paratracheal (scanty)

Betula sp., 375X

Birch

Other example:
Acer spp.

e. Paratracheal (vasicentric)

Fraxinus americana, 200X

White ash

Other examples:
Umbellularia californica
Diospyros virginiana

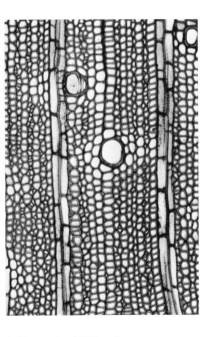

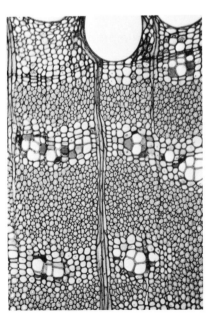

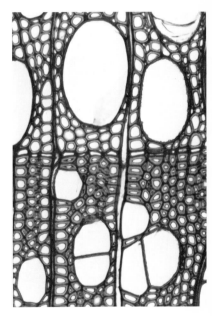

f. Paratracheal (aliform)

Sassafras albidum, 125X

Sassafras

Other examples:
Fraxinus spp.
Umbellularia californica

g. Paratracheal (confluent)

Gleditsia triancanthos,

Honeylocust

Other example:
Fraxinus americana (latewood)

h. Marginal (terminal)

Populus deltoides,

Eastern cottonwood

Other examples:
Salix spp.
Liriodendron tulipifera

Figure 22 (continued).

COMMENTS ON HARDWOOD IDENTIFICATION

The following observations have been assembled as background information which may prove useful in identifying some of the more common hardwoods.

Oaks

Once sawn into lumber, the oaks are separable only to groups: the red oaks and the white oaks. The *most accurate* separation is made by comparing the summerwood pores and noting the thickness of the vessel wall, the angularity of pore outline, the pore abundance and the pore size. The red oak group has larger, more rounded pores with thick walls and the pores are fewer in number.

Ashes

Commercial white ash usually is separated from black (brown) ash on the basis of being more lustrous as well as stronger. Generally white ash has wider growth rings than black ash. Frequently black ash has growth rings so narrow that the latewood is barely visible.

Maples

Like the oaks, the maples are separated into groups for commercial purposes. These are the hard maple and the soft maple. The hard maples will show rays of two distinct sizes and will have a lustrous appearance. Soft maples have rays intergrading in size and are essentially non-lustrous. Other maples such as bigleaf, box elder and the exotic species may vary somewhat in color of heartwood and in size of elements but are extremely difficult to identify.

Dogwood

Most frequently confused with hard maple, this wood is identified by its pinkish or flesh-colored cast in the sapwood, solitary pores in part, and apotracheal banded parenchyma in the latewood. The latter feature is difficult to see.

Black Locust

This wood is separated from Osage orange by having distinct pore outlines in the earlywood. Osage orange has indistinct outlines and, in addition, contains a water-soluble dye which will produce a yellow color when shavings are soaked in water.

Mulberry

Mulberry is separated from black locust and Osage orange by several features. First, in contrast with the other two species, the pores are not completely occluded with tyloses. It has abundant latewood pores in nest-like groups and usually in a loose, ulmiform pattern. In addition, whitish deposits are commonly found in a few of the vessels.

Hickories

The pecan hickories usually are softer, more semiring-porous, and the heartwoods more reddish brown than the true hickories. Several authorities mention that the apotracheal-banded parenchyma extends more deeply into the earlywood in pecan.

Elms

The elms are variable enough so that it is difficult to distinguish them in all instances. This is true particularly of the hard elms and American elm.

MICROSCOPIC FEATURES—HARDWOODS

Many diagnostic features of hardwoods may be observed with the unaided eye or with a hand lens. These would be classed as gross characteristics or hand lens features, while those beyond the resolving power of these optical systems are microscopic features. As mentioned previously, overlap can be expected as structural features vary in size between species. The structures discussed and illustrated in this section are generally too small to be seen without the aid of a light microscope.

Rays

Among the microscopic features to be examined in hardwoods are ray composition, ray-vessel pitting, and presence of oil cells. The latter are rare in occurrence in native hardwoods and are restricted to the members of the Lauraceae: *Sassafras* and *Umbellularia*. Oil cells usually appear as large, tear-shaped cells in the margins of rays. Occasionally they are found in strand parenchyma. (See Figure 23.)

Normal rays may be composed of all procumbent cells, all upright cells, or of both upright and procumbent cells. If all cells are alike the rays are called homocellular and if both shapes of cells are present in a ray the rays are heterocellular. Ray composition has not been used to any great extent as a diagnostic feature with native hardwoods but has wide application in tropical hardwoods. Both tangential and radial surfaces should be examined to determine ray composition. Table 5 lists the ray composition of native hardwoods. Figures 24 and 25 illustrate types of ray composition.

The pit pairs connecting rays and vessels are termed ray-vessel pitting. Their appearance is often quite distinctive and thus they provide a useful diagnostic feature. Unfortunately, ray-vessel pitting has not been widely used in the identification of commercial woods. Generally they are described as being similar or dissimilar to the intervessel pitting. When dissimilar, the pitting may be bordered in appearance, or simple. The pit outline may be rounded, oval,

a. Radial section, 150X

Figure 23. Oil cells present in the rays of sassafras, *Sassafras albidum,* as observed in radial and tangential views. Oil cells may also be found in *Umbellularia sp.*

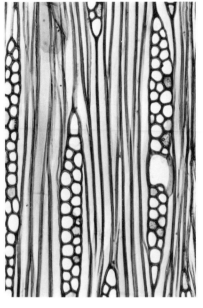

b. Tangential section, 140X

Table 5

RAY COMPOSITION OF NATIVE HARDWOODS			
Essentially Homocellular		Heterocellular and Homocellular	
Acer	Gymnocladus	Arbutus	Magnolia
Aesculus	Lithocarpus	Carpinus	Maclura
(Ailanthus)	Maclura	Carya	Morus
(Albizzia)	(Melia)	Celtis	Nyssa
Alnus	(Paulownia)	Cercis	Ostrya
Betula	Platanus	Cladrastis	Oxydendron
Castanea	Quercus	Cornus	Prunus
Castanopsis	Rhamnus	Fagus	Sassafras
Catalpa	Robinia	Ilex	Robinia
Diospyros	Populus	Juglans	Umbellularia
Fraxinus	Tilia	Liquidambar	
Gleditsia	Ulmus	Liriodendron	

(   ) = Naturalized species

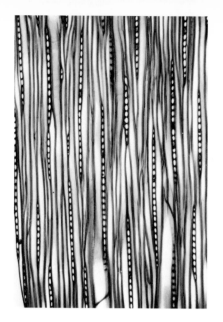
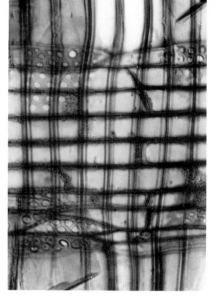

Tangential section,
80X

Radial section,
310X

Uniseriate homocellular rays
Populus deltoides
Eastern cottonwood

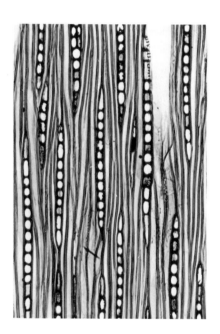
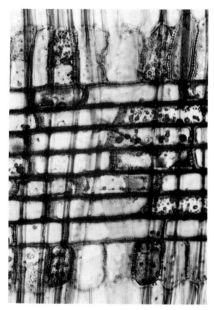

Tangential section,
125X

Radial section,
310X

Uniseriate heterocellular rays
Salix nigra
Black willow

Figure 24. The structure of uniseriate rays in hardwoods. *Note:* In the examples shown here, all of the cells in the homocellular ray are of the procumbent type. In the heterocellular ray, the marginal cells are upright and those in the body of the ray are procumbent.

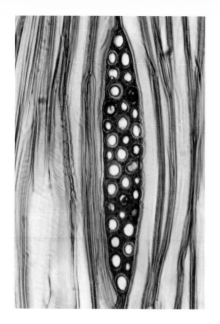

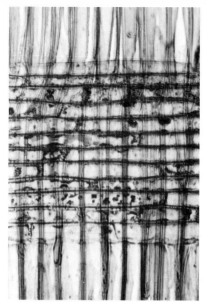

Multiseriate homocellular rays
Tangential section, 310X
Acer saccharinum
Silver maple

Multiseriate homocellular rays
Radial section, 310X
Acer rubrum
Red maple

Other examples: *Ulmus spp., Betula spp.*

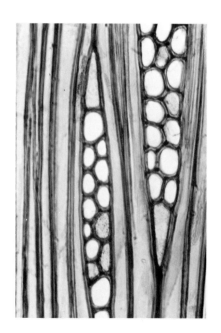

Multiseriate heterocellular rays
Tangential section, 310X

Multiseriate heterocellular rays
Radial section, 310X

Sassafras albidum, Sassafras

Other example: *Celtis spp.*

Figure 25. The structure of multiseriate rays in hardwoods.

or elongated. In some instances the pitting may be restricted to the last few rows of marginal cells or to the upright cells of heterocellular rays. Some examples of ray-vessel pitting are shown in Figure 26, and Table 6 classifies the type of ray-vessel pitting generally found in the hardwood species.

Table 6

RAY-VESSEL PITTING OF HARDWOODS				
Similar to Intervessel Pitting		Essentially Simple	Simple to Bordered	
Acer	Gymnocladus	Aesculus	Arbutus	Magnolia
(Albizzia)	Ilex	Celtis	(Ailanthus)	Morus
Alnus	Juglans	Maclura	Carpinus	Ostrya
Betula	(Melia)	Salix	Castanea	Populus
Carya	Nyssa	Umbellularia	Castanopsis	Quercus
Catalpa	(Paulownia)		Fagus	Robinia
Cladrastis	Platanus		Liquidambar	Sassafras
Cornus	Rhamnus		Liriodendron	Ulmus
Diospyros				
Fraxinus				
Gleditsia				

(   ) = Naturalized species

Aggregate rays were discussed as macroscopic features. If a microscope is used to examine the tissue, the composition of the ray, with both longitudinal and ray elements, will be more obvious. *Alnus* and *Carpinus* exhibit aggregate rays while *Lithocarpus* and some *Quercus* species will contain aggregate rays in addition to the broad oak-type rays. See Figure 17 for illustrations of aggregate rays.

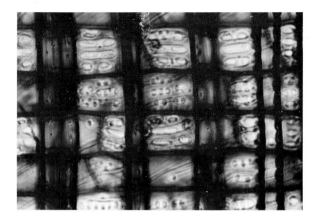

a. Simple and elongated to bordered
Magnolia grandiflora, 375X
Evergreen magnolia
Other examples:
Aesculus octandra
Sassafras albidum

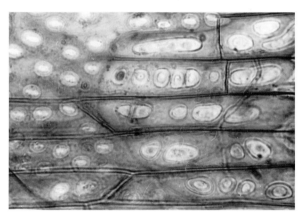

b. Simple to bordered, variable in shape and size
Castanea dentata, 625X
American chestnut
Other examples:
Quercus spp.
Ulmus spp.
Morus rubra

c. Similar to intervessel pitting
Acer saccharinum, 575X
Silver maple
Other examples:
Betula spp.
Prunus serotina
Ilex opaca

Figure 26. Ray-vessel pitting in hardwoods.

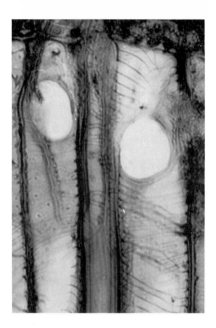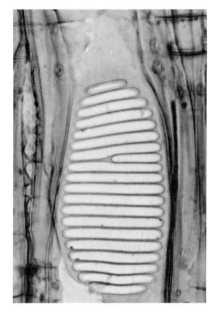

a. Simple perforations

Ulmus fulva, 287X

Red elm

Other examples:
Quercus spp.
Acer spp.
Carya spp.

b. Scalariform perforations

Liquidambar styraciflua, 375X

Redgum

Other examples:
Betula spp.
Liriodendron sp.
Alnus rubra

Figure 27. Typical simple and scalariform perforations in the vessels of hardwoods.

Vessel Element Perforations

A perforation, either simple or scalariform, is the opening which occurs usually at the junction of two vessel elements allowing for free movement of liquids and gases in the sapwood. Although they are in the minority, scalariform perforations are relatively common in temperate zone hardwoods. *Liquidambar, Liriodendron, Ilex, Nyssa, Cornus, Betula, Alnus, Ostrya, Carpinus, Magnolia grandiflora, Oxydendron,* and *Arbutus* have exclusively scalariform perforations. *Fagus, Platanus,* and *Sassafras* have both simple and scalariform perforations with the latter usually occurring in the latewood vessel elements. *Castanea* will show scalariform perforations rarely and the juvenile wood of *Magnolia acuminata* will have some of the vessel elements with scalariform perforations.

Figures 27a and 27b are photomicrographs of typical simple and scalariform perforations, while Figures 28a and 28b show scanning microscope views of similar structures.

Intervessel Pitting

The pitting which occurs between adjacent vessel elements is called intervessel pitting. Normally, it is most abundant on the tangential surfaces of the elements since they are in contact most often in this plane. Occasionally, when the vessel distribution is mostly solitary, it is necessary to examine the areas of overlapping vessel element ends above and below the perforations. These areas would be visible on the radial surface.

Intervessel pitting varies as to shape and size of individual pit outline and aperture, arrangement, and spacing. Shape of pit outline and arrangement of pits are the most useful diagnostic features.

Pit shape (outline) varies from round to angular to oval to linear (Figure 29). Round and oval are the most common. If the pits are crowded, they tend to become angular. Occasionally, pits coalesce early in their formation and become elongated. Such pits are described as linear. A series of linear pits arranged in a vertical row gives the arrangement known as scalariform pitting (Figure 29c).

Three arrangements of pitting are recognized: alternate, in which the pits are arranged diagonally on the vessel element; opposite, where the pits form horizontal rows; and scalariform, where enlarged, linear pits in vertical rows give the appearance of a ladder-like formation. Frequently the linear pits will extend across the vessel element wall. Alternate pitting arrangement is most common and is the rule in most hardwoods. Opposite arrangement is rare enough that it is an excellent diagnostic feature. Among our native woods, yellowpoplar, redgum, tupelo gum, holly (in part), and dogwood (in part) have opposite intervessel pit arrangment (Figure 29).

Scalariform pit arrangement is even more rare than the opposite arrangement. *Magnolia* spp., redgum (in part), and dogwood (in part) are about the only native woods that show this pattern.

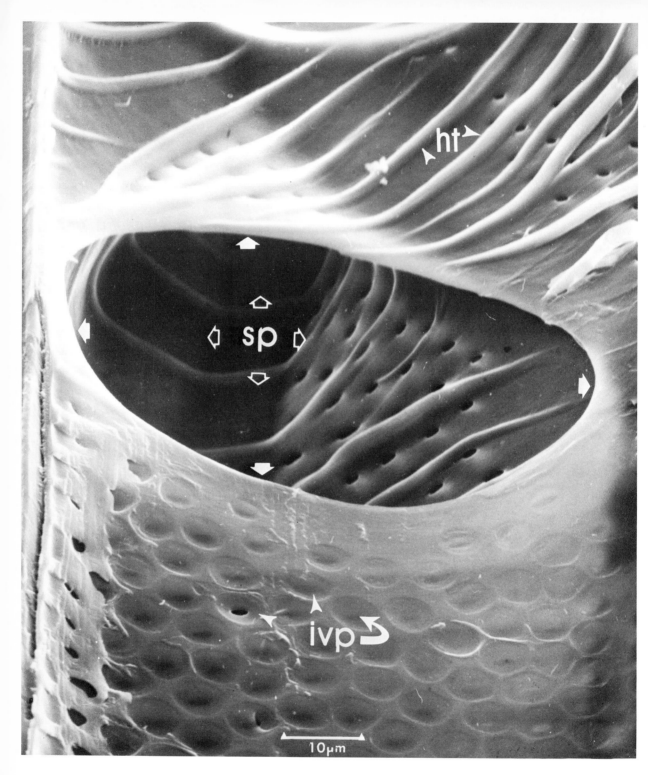

Figure 28a. Scanning electron micrograph of bass-wood, *Tilia americana*, showing a simple perforation (sp) between two vessel elements. Intervessel pitting (ivp) and helical thickenings (ht) are other prominent features of this micrograph.

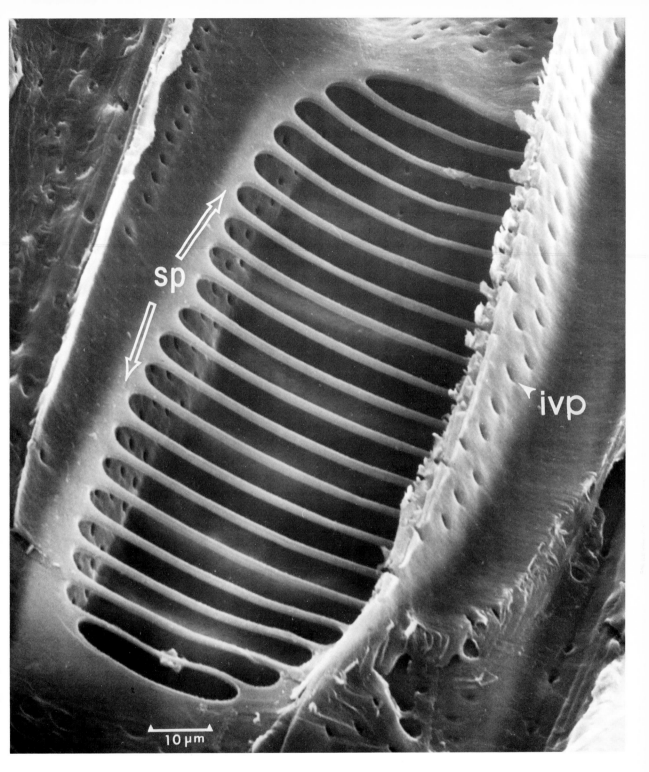

Figure 28b. Perforations between vessel elements may have elaborate structure in some species. In this scanning electron micrograph of red alder, *Alnus rubra,* the ladder-like bars of a scalariform perforation plate (sp) are prominent. Also there is intervessel pitting (ivp) visible.

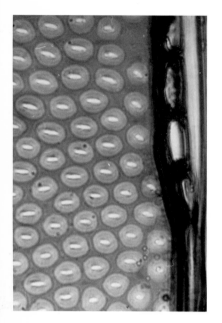 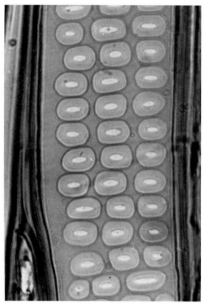 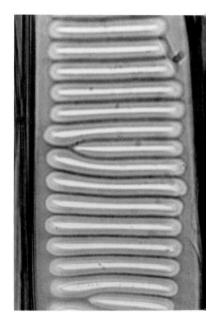

a. Alternate intervessel pitting

Populus deltoides, 700X

Eastern cottonwood

Other examples:
Acer spp.
Betula spp.

b. Opposite intervessel pitting

Liriodendron tulipifera, 700X

Yellowpoplar

Other examples:
Liquidambar sp.
Nyssa spp.

c. Scalariform intervessel pitting

Magnolia acuminata, 750X

Cucumbertree

Other examples:
Magnolia grandiflora
Cornus spp. (in part)

Figure 29. Intervessel pitting arrangement in hardwoods.

Vestured Intervessel Pitting

The woods of black locust, honeylocust, Kentucky coffeetree, and yellowwood will have alternate intervessel pitting with outgrowths in the pit chamber and into the pit apertures. These structures are readily seen with the scanning electron microscope (Figure 30), but are near the limit of resolution with a light microscope in many cases. Caution must be advised in using this evidence until sufficient experience has been developed to recognize the structures shown in Figure 30 as "vestures."

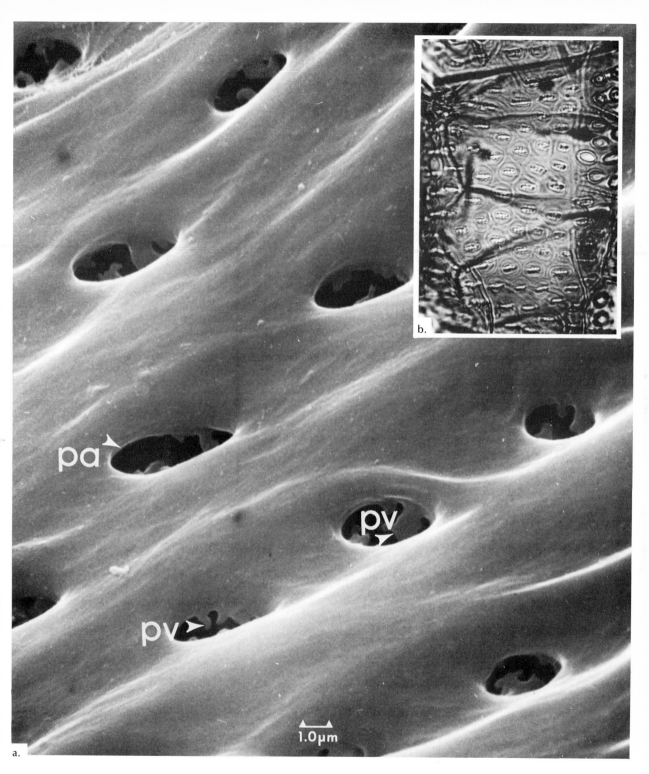

Figure 30. Vestured intervessel pitting occurs in only a few native hardwoods, although it is much more common in tropical wood species. A vestured pit contains outgrowths from the pit chamber wall or the pit aperture. These projections are near the limit of resolution of the light microscope as can be judged from the photomicrograph (Figure 30 b). In a scanning electron micrograph (Figure 30 a) the pit apertures (pa) and the pit vestures (pv) are clearly resolved. The photomicrograph is a tangential section of black locust, *Robinia pseudoacacia,* and the SEM is a view of a vessel wall from Kentucky coffeetree, *Gymnocladus dioicus.*

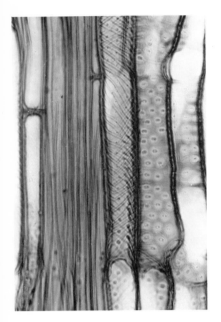
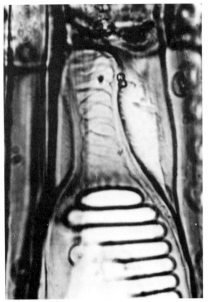

a. Helical (spiral) thickenings in vessels
Ulmus americana, 285X
American elm
Other example:
Acer spp.

b. Helical (spiral) thickenings in ligulate tips
Liquidambar styraciflua, 750X
Redgum
Other example:
Nyssa spp.

c. Helical (spiral) thickenings in fibers
Arbutus menziesii, 310X
Madrone
Other example:
Ilex opaca

Figure 31. Helical thickenings in the vessels and fiber of hardwoods.

Helical (Spiral) Thickening

Helical thickenings are much more common among temperate zone hardwoods than in either tropical hardwoods or coniferous woods. With a few exceptions, helical thickenings, when present, are restricted to vessel elements. The thickenings may be present in all vessel elements, in latewood elements only, or be restricted to the ligulate tips of the vessel elements. Table 7 lists the occurrence of helical thickenings among the common hardwoods. Figure 31 may be referred to for typical examples of this anatomical structure as seen with the scanning electron microscope as well as with the light microscope.

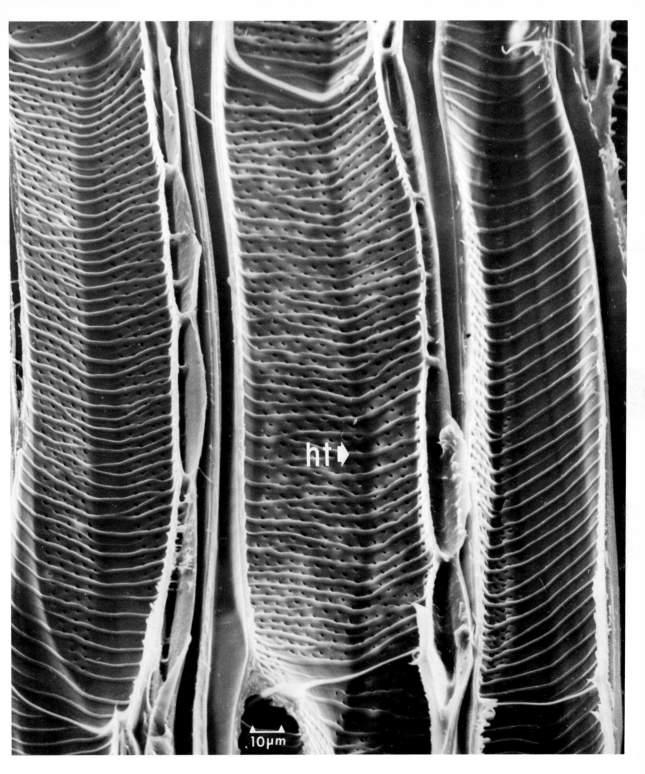

d. Scanning electron micrograph of basswood, *Tilia americana*, whose vessels are characteristically lined with helical thickenings (ht). Note the intervessel pitting between the thickenings. Three vessels are included in this micrograph.

Figure 31 (continued).

Table 7

Occurrence of Helical Thickenings in Common Hardwoods				
Sporadic or Inconspicuous	Occurring in all Vessel Elements	Occurring in Latewood Vessel Elements Only	Occurring in Vessels and Fibers	Restricted to Vessel Tips
Aesculus	*Acer*	*Catalpa*	*Arbutus*	*Liquidambar*
Oxydendron	*Arbutus*	*Celtis*	*Ilex*	*Nyssa*
	Carpinus	*Cladrastis*		
	Ilex	*Gleditsia*		
	M. grandiflora	*Gymnocladus*		
	(Melia)	*Maclura*		
	Ostrya	*Morus*		
	Oxydendron	*Robinia*		
	Prunus	*Ulmus*		
	Tilia			

(   ) = Naturalized species.

Vasicentric Tracheids

These unusual tracheids are restricted to members of the Fagaceae and the *Fraxinus* species. A photomicrograph of a characteristic group of vasicentric tracheids is included as Figure 32.

Vascular Tracheids

As with vasicentric tracheids, these elements are not common among native commercial hardwoods. They are limited to woods of the Ulmaceae family. Since they are extremely difficult to differentiate from small vessel elements in sectioned wood, they are of limited value in diagnosis. See Figure 33 for an example taken from *Ulmus fulva*.

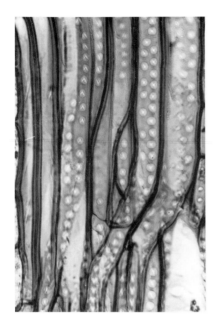

Quercus macrocarpa, 285X
Bur oak
Other example:
Castanea sp.

Figure 32. Vasicentric tracheids of hardwoods.

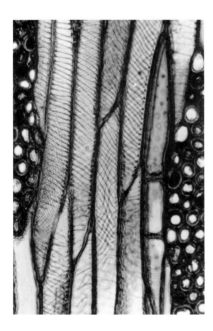

Ulmus fulva, 290X
Red elm
Other example:
Celtis spp.

Figure 33. Vascular tracheids of hardwoods.

Tyloses

Tyloses are membranous materials that fill or occlude the lumens of vessel elements and, occasionally, other prosenchymatous elements. They result from the protrusion of a pit membrane and growth of protoplasm into the empty vessel lumen under growth or other pressures exerted by a living parenchyma cell. These neighboring living cells may be longitudinal or ray elements.

One widely held theory is that the diameter of the pit involved in tylosis formation must be a minimum of 8 to 10 micrometers. Smaller pits evidently can resist the pressures involved. Tyloses develop at the time of heartwood formation in the tree or as a result of injury. The heartwood of most temperate zone woods contains tyloses in varying amounts. Black locust and Osage orange have essentially all of the earlywood pores in the heartwood occluded with tyloses; white oak and mulberry have numerous tyloses. Black cherry, maple, Kentucky coffeetree, yellowwood, honeylocust, redbud, buckthorn, basswood, dogwood, and sourwood normally do not show evidence of tyloses. Other woods exhibit tyloses in varying amounts. Except for black locust and Osage orange, this feature should be used cautiously as its occurrence in the others may vary with growth conditions.

The three-dimensional nature of tyloses is more readily observed on scanning electron micrographs (Figure 34), but photomicrographs such as Figure 35 show that the light microscope provides adequate resolution for the evaluation of tylosis development.

Gum

There is a companion theory that suggests that if pit diameters are too small for tylosis formation, often there will be the deposition of gum in the vessels. Adjacent parenchyma cells would still be considered the source of such material. Black cherry, maple, and honeylocust are three common woods in which gum deposits occur in vessels. Figure 36 indicates that there should be very little difficulty in separating tyloses from gum as structural features.

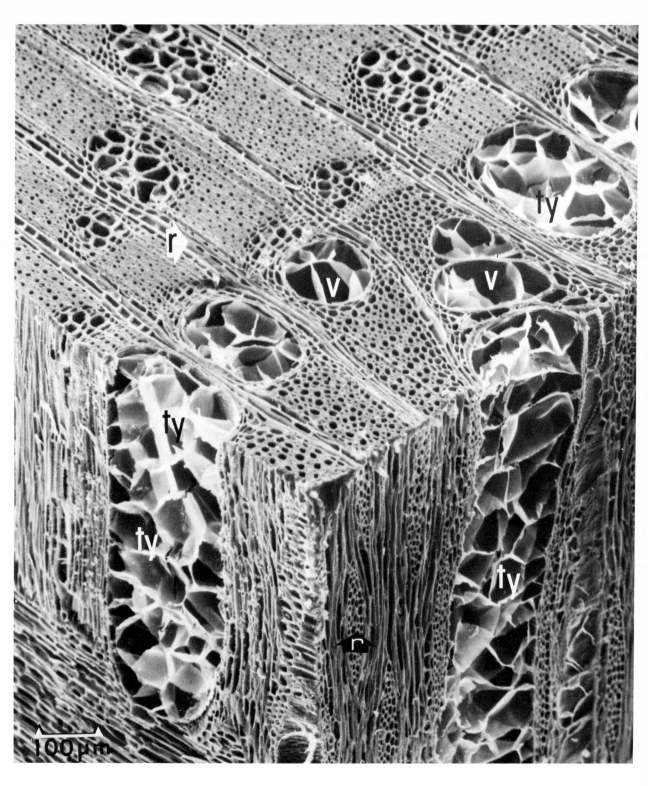

Figure 34. In some hardwoods tyloses are found consistently in the vessels. Among these species, black locust, *Robinia pseudoacacia*, is a good example. In this scanning electron micrograph the vessels (v) are plugged by these membranous structures, tyloses (t). Tyloses arise as outgrowths from ray or longitudinal parenchyma cells adjoining vessels. The pit membrane of an active cell proliferates into the empty vessel and grows as a bud or into a larger balloon-like structure. When this is repeated from many pits, tyloses can form a frothy looking mass in a vessel.

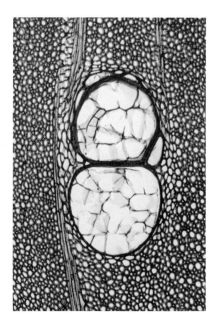

Figure 35. Photomicrograph of cross-section of black locust, *Robinia pseudoacacia,* showing the nature of tyloses in the vessels. 95X

Fiber Tracheids

Fiber tracheids intergrade with libriform fibers (see below). Those with conspicuous bordered pits are useful in identification. Woods whose fibers show bordered pits conspicuously include: *Liquidambar, Nyssa, Ilex, Magnolia, Liriodendron,* and *Cornus.* Examine the photomicrograph in Figure 37 to see the striking difference in pitting.

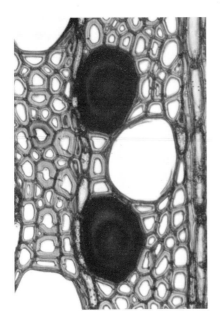

Figure 36. Photomicrograph of cross-section of black cherry, *Prunus serotina*, with gum deposits in the vessels. 310X

Libriform Fibers

The characteristics that identify a fiber as a libriform fiber are tenuous and may be very difficult for the beginner to use with confidence. As a consequence, this feature is used only as a last resort and then in conjunction with other features. Both septations and gelatinous layers occur in "fibers." Septations are characteristic of certain species mostly tropical while gelatinous layers usually indicate tension (reaction) wood. See Figure 37 for graphic evidence of structural features of these cell types.

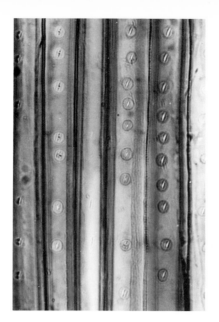

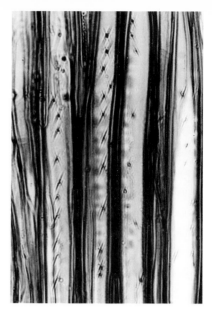

a. Fiber tracheids (t,r)

Liquidambar styraciflua, 375X

Redgum

Other examples:
Nyssa spp.
Ilex spp.

b. Libriform fibers, normal (t,r)

Fraxinus nigra, 375X

Black ash

Other examples:
Umbellularia californica
Gymnocladus dioicus

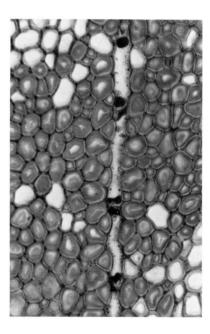

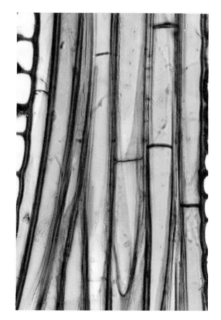

c. Libriform fibers, gelatinous

Quercus sp., 310X

Oak

Other examples:
Morus rubra
Celtis spp.

d. Libriform fibers, septate

Swietenia sp., 310X

Mahogany (tropical)

Other examples:
Umbellularia californica

Figure 37. Fiber tracheids, libriform fibers, gelatinous fibers, and septate fibers in hardwoods.

Crystals

Crystals may be present in many hardwoods. They are of minor diagnostic significance. Their presence may be helpful, but the absence of crystals may be due to chance. One interesting note is that black walnut usually will show rhomboidal crystals in the longitudinal parenchyma, while butternut will not. An example of crystals in black walnut is included as Figure 38. The analysis of crystals such as those shown in Figure 38 has become a somewhat simpler process through the use of the scanning electron microscope and energy dispersive x-ray analysis (EDXA) which can be interfaced with it.

Crystals in ray or longitudinal parenchyma

Juglans nigra, 310X

Black walnut

Other examples:
Carya spp.
Fagus grandifolia

Figure 38. Crystals in the parenchyma cells of hardwoods.

For example, Figure 39a is a scanning electron micrograph of a specimen of black walnut wood containing crystals. It was made in the so-called backscattered electron or primary electron mode. The crystals are detected very readily by this technique.

While preparing the scanning electron micrograph of Figure 39a, the EDXA equipment can be used simultaneously to collect characteristic x-rays from the specimen. Figure 39b is a photograph of the x-ray spectrum produced from this sample and there is a major peak which is readily identified as calcium (Ca).

Using the element mapping capability of this instrumentation, it is possible to collect only the Ca x-rays and to utilize them as illustrated in Figure 39c. The same crystals as those in Figure 39a are thus shown to contain calcium as one of the principal elements.

Silica

In the normal growth process, some trees grown on appropriate sites evidently adsorb salts (in solution) that are ultimately deposited in the cells as silica. Frequently this is in the form of "sand," but other forms are also found. While such deposits are not common in domestic commercial woods, silica is found widely in tropical hardwoods and is the source of machining problems in many cases. The SEM and EDXA technique described above for the analysis of crystals in wood works equally well for silica.

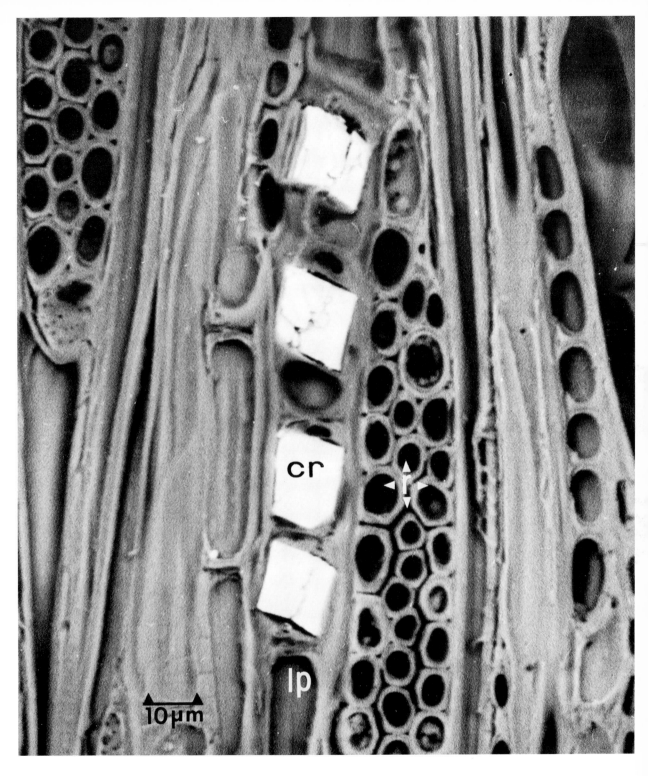

Figure 39a. Scanning electron micrograph, back-scattered electron mode, showing crystals (cr) in longitudinal parenchyma cells (lp) of black walnut, as in the photomicrograph of Figure 38. The ends of rays (r) make up a large portion of this tangential surface view.

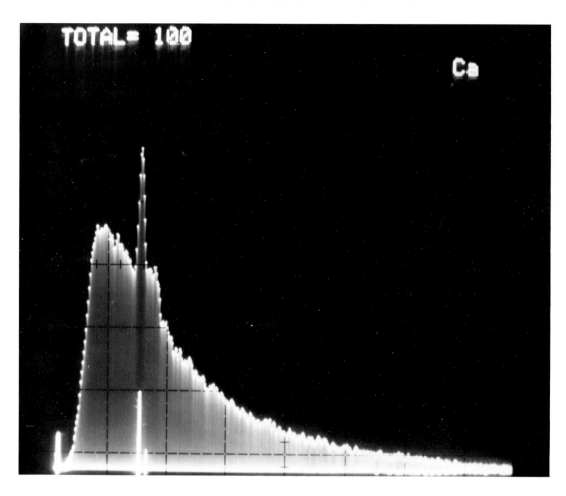

Figure 39b. Energy dispersive x-ray analysis (EDXA) spectrum of the specimen shown in Figure 39a.   The major peak shown is calcium (Ca).

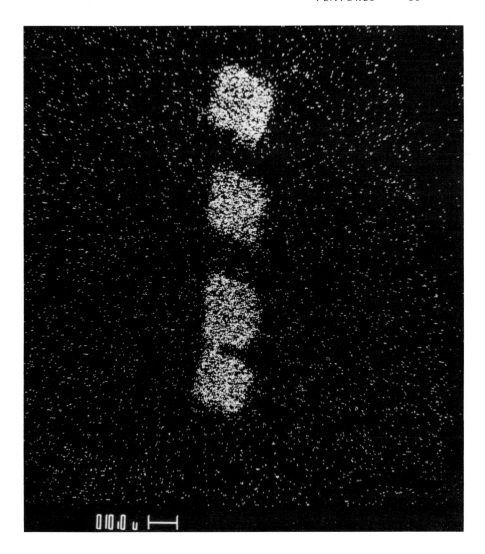

Figure 39c. An element map for calcium (Ca) covering the exact area of the specimen shown in Figure 39a. This indicates that calcium is a major constituent of the crystals found in the longitudinal parenchyma cells.

MACROSCOPIC FEATURES—SOFTWOODS

The nature of the macroscopic features useful in separating the native softwoods is rather different than that of hardwoods. Perhaps the differences might be described in terms of subtleties of color, odor, texture, and gross characteristics of wood. Positive identification is not always possible and often it is necessary to resort to microscopic features. As with hardwoods, there are areas of overlap between macro- and microscopic features. These will become obvious from the discussion and the illustrations.

Resin Canals

Hardwoods do not have resin canals (although gum canals occur in some woods), but a few genera among the softwoods have them as normal features. Traumatic longitudinal resin canals are found as a result of injury in some woods that do not normally exhibit this structural feature.

Resin canals are present in *Pinus, Picea, Larix,* and *Pseudotsuga.* They are more abundant and usually larger in *Pinus* than in the other genera. Resin canals may be identified by small holes or dots on the cross-section and tangential section or by the presence of occasional, large (fusiform) rays. The rays of the wood will appear to be of two sizes in the latter instance. Figure 40 is a scanning electron micrograph illustrating normal resin canals.

The size of resin canals varies in *Pinus* species. They are largest in *P. lambertiana* and *P. ponderosa.* Relatively small canals (for *Pinus*) are characteristic of *P. resinosa* and *P. contorta* var. *latifolia.*

Resin Canal Surface Streaks

In *Pinus,* dark streaks are frequently visible along the grain on the surface of boards. These mark the position of longitudinal resin canals, the resin of which may be colored or have caught dust to cause the streak. Such streaks are generally not visible in *Picea, Larix,* and *Pseudotsuga* since the canals are smaller and the resin is not as copious.

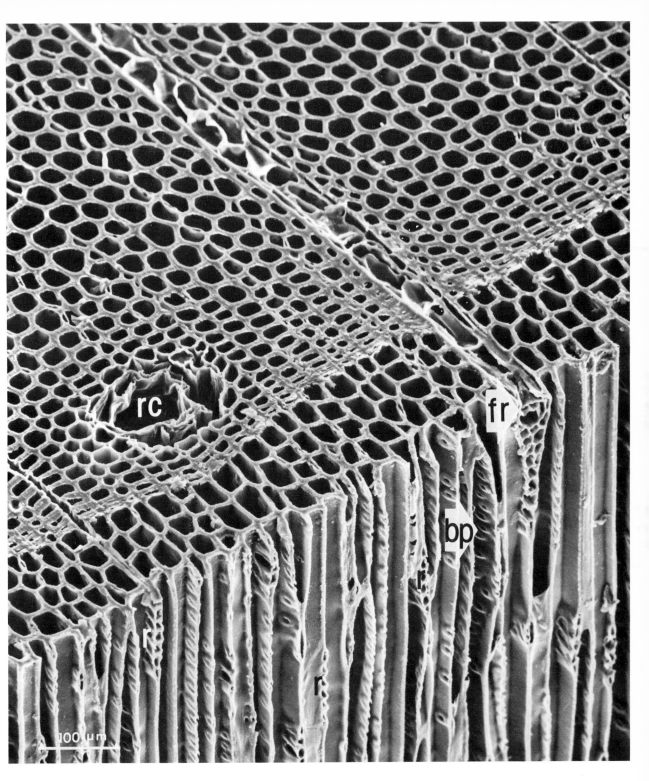

Figure 40. Scanning electron micrograph of the wood of eastern white pine, *Pinus strobus*, a species having normal resin canals (rc). On the tangential surface the canals can be found incorporated into a fusiform ray (fr). In this particular sample, the fusiform ray was cut so that it is visible on the transverse surface as well. Other rays (r) and bordered pits (bp) are labeled.

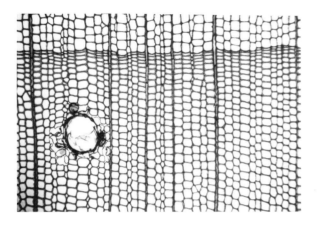

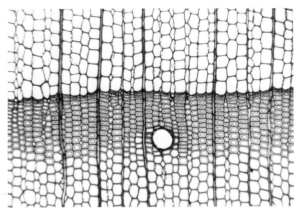

a. Gradual transition from earlywood
to latewood

Pinus monticola, 70X

Western white pine

Other examples:
Picea spp. (except Sitka spruce)
Pinus spp. (soft pines only)

b. Abrupt transition from earlywood to
latewood

Larix occidentalis, 40X

Western larch

Other examples:
Pinus spp. (hard pines only)
Pseudotsuga menziesii

Figure 41. Earlywood-latewood transition may be gradual as in (a) or
abrupt as in (b).

Earlywood-Latewood Transition

In the soft pines, (*P. lambertiana, P. strobus, P. monti-cola*) the transition from earlywood to latewood is gradual; the reverse holds true for the hard pines. This feature is best seen with the naked eye on the moist, transverse surface. Very slow-growth *P. ponderosa* from California, with very narrow bands of latewood, frequently resembles soft pine and was sold at one time as California white pine. Some shortleaf pine will also have narrow bands of latewood. In both instances the narrow latewood band will show sharp gradations on both sides with careful hand lens examination. Figure 41 shows the differences in earlywood-latewood transition between soft and hard pines.

In *Picea* the transition from earlywood to latewood is usually gradual. *Picea engelmannii,* which grows at high altitudes in the Rocky Mountains, is somewhat of an exception to the rule. The transition from early- to latewood is abrupt in *Larix* and *Pseudotsuga*.

Dimple Marks

The split tangential surface of lodgepole pine characteristically has small depressions or undulations which resemble dimples. Occasionally other western yellow pines and the spruces will show dimpling.

COMMENTS ON SOFTWOOD IDENTIFICATION

In identifying the softwoods, the following observations may be helpful by highlighting certain features and emphasizing differences between woods that are difficult to separate.

Spruces vs. Western Yellow Pines

The spruces differ from the western yellow pines in that the summerwood is not accentuated and the transition from earlywood to latewood is gradual. The lateral surfaces of the spruces are lustrous. The pines have a strong, resinous odor while the spruces do not.

In distinguishing lodgepole pine from the other western yellow pines, when dimple marks are suspect, the size of the resin canals may be helpful. In lodgepole pine the resin canals are small (for a pine) in contrast to the large canals of the others.

Heartwood of Soft Pines

The heartwood of *Pinus lambertiana* is light brown to pale, reddish brown; the heartwoods of *P. strobus* and *P. monticola* are darker (deep reddish brown).

The Spruces vs. Balsam Fir

Red, white, and black spruce cannot be separated either by gross characteristics or minute features. Eastern spruce (any of the above) is usually pale yellowish white on a fresh cut surface and possesses distinct luster (more than pine). Balsam fir (*Abies balsamea*) resembles eastern spruce in color and luster; the wood is heavier than spruce as it comes from the tree because it contains more moisture, but it is lighter when oven dry. The best feature used to separate eastern spruce from balsam fir is the presence of resin canals in spruce. These usually appear as tiny white dots in the outer part of the growth ring. Engelmann spruce (*Picea engelmannii*) often is considered comparable to eastern spruces which it resembles in color and luster. However, it usually has a relatively abrupt transition from earlywood to latewood.

Sitka spruce (*Picea sitchensis*) is distinct from eastern spruce. The heartwood is darker (pale brown with a pinkish or purplish cast) and the resin canals are larger. Sitka spruce is also a coarser-textured wood. It is sometimes mistaken for soft pine.

Douglas-fir

Pseudotsuga menziesii has a wide geographical and altitudinal range. Consequently the wood is quite variable in color and ring width. The heartwood ranges from yellowish or pale reddish yellow (narrow-ringed stock) to orange-red or deep red (wide-ringed stock). The longitudinal resin canals may be scattered or in tangential rows of 5 to 30, resembling traumatic canals but located in the outer portion of the ring. Douglas-fir wood has a characteristic resinous odor when fresh, different from that of pine, and is unpleasant to some persons. The presence of resin canals along with consistent helical thickenings in the earlywood tracheids is positive identification for *Pseudotsuga*.

Eastern vs. Western Larch

The heartwood of eastern larch is yellowish brown (russet) without a reddish tinge. The heartwood of western larch is reddish brown but not as red as the red grades of Douglas-fir. Eastern larch frequently has wide rings and rings variable in width, even in small samples (second-growth trees). In western larch the rings are usually narrow and quite uniform in width (large, overmature trees). Western larch is much coarser-textured than eastern larch. The resin canals of both woods are extremely small and sporadic in distribution. Consequently, they are difficult to find. Examine the cross-section carefully for two different sizes of rays (fusiform and uniseriate) if in doubt. Refer to Figure 40 for a scanning electron microscopic view of ray types in conifers.

Hemlock vs. Western True Firs

The *Tsuga* species are difficult to separate from the western *Abies*. In general, the rings of the firs are wider (intolerant, fast-growing trees), and the transition from early-wood to latewood is more gradual. The width of the late-wood may be just as great, however. The final check is by use of the minute anatomy. Ray tracheids are present in *Tsuga* and essentially absent in *Abies*. See Figure 44 for photomicrographs of rays and compare them for the presence and absence of ray tracheids. Hemlock wood (particularly eastern hemlock) appears to be more brittle and splintery than fir wood and has a dry feel in seasoned material.

Eastern vs. Western Hemlock

The wood of eastern hemlock is of poorer quality than that of western hemlock. Since eastern hemlock is a tolerant tree and recovers from suppression, and since most eastern hemlock comes from second-growth trees, the ring width, even in a small sample, may be quite variable. The ring width in western hemlock is usually more uniform because the wood comes from large, overmature trees. Therefore, western hemlock is more even-textured than eastern hemlock. Traumatic resin canals occur in western hemlock, but they are seldom found in eastern hemlock.

Western True Firs

The woods of the western firs cannot be separated with certainty, even with the aid of a microscope.

Redwood vs. Baldcypress

Redwood and baldcypress are the coarsest-textured coniferous woods considered in this manual. The openings (cell lumens) of the earlywood tracheids are readily seen on the transverse surface with the aid of a hand lens. Both woods have strands of longitudinal parenchyma which are visible along the grain with a hand lens because of the dark deposits in the cells (beaded parenchyma).

Redwood is easily separated from baldcypress because of its light red to deep reddish brown heartwood in contrast to the heartwood of cypress which is rarely reddish. Redwood is dry, brittle, and splintery; baldcypress has a greasy feel, usually a rancid odor, and is not as brittle or as splintery as redwood. Western and eastern larch also are somewhat greasy to the touch and occasionally are confused for baldcypress. However, they contain resin canals.

Three grades of baldcypress are recognized in the trade: (a) red cypress from old, overmature trees grown in deep swamps has very dark heartwood; (b) yellow cypress with lighter heartwood; (c) white cypress with little infiltration in the heartwood (from young, second-growth trees). White cypress may have no appreciable odor.

The Cedars

The cedars (Cupressaceae) have pleasantly scented woods, and the scents vary according to species. Although very difficult to describe, the scents are important diagnostic features in separating these woods.

The heartwood of arborvitae (northern white cedar) (*Thuja occidentalis*) is a uniform straw-brown (without a pinkish cast); that of western red cedar (*Thuja plicata*) is pinkish to reddish brown, fading to a uniform dull brown. Western red cedar is coarser textured than arborvitae, a feature that can be seen with a hand lens. Neither of these woods have much "body"; that is, they are light and soft. Western red cedar has a pronounced latewood band with abrupt transition. It has a sweet, chocolate-like odor.

Atlantic white cedar (*Chamaecyparis thyoides*) is sometimes confused with *Thuja occidentalis*. The scent is different and the heartwood has a pinkish cast. The wood is rubbery under a knife and not as brittle as northern white cedar. The wet cross-section of Atlantic white cedar normally will show reddish zone lines resulting from concentrations or tangential bands of longitudinal parenchyma.

The western species of *Chamaecyparis*, *C. lawsoniana*, and *C. nootkatensis* are distinct from the eastern *C. thyoides*. Port Orford cedar (*C. lawsoniana*) is yellowish-white to pale yellowish-brown, with a characteristic pungent, ginger-like odor when freshly cut. Alaska yellow cedar (*C. nootkatensis*) is a uniform light clear yellow with the odor of raw potatoes. The rings in Alaska yellow cedar usually are narrower than in samples of Port Orford cedar.

Incense cedar (*Libocedrus decurrens*) is a firm, medium-hard coniferous wood with nearly as much "body" as eastern red cedar. The heartwood is a uniform reddish brown and is duller than eastern red cedar. Incense cedar has a spicy, acrid taste and a pungent odor. It differs from western red cedar in odor, uniformity of texture, and in having more "body."

Eastern red cedar (*Juniperus virginiana*) is readily distinguished from other cedars by the color of its heartwood (purplish rose-red). The wood is firmer than the others. It is the premier pencil wood, but it is used only in limited quantities due to lack of supply. Incense cedar is used in its place. Eastern red cedar has a higher infiltration content than the other cedars.

Pacific Yew

Among the native softwoods, Pacific yew (*Taxus brevifolia*) is distinctive because of its bright orange to rose-red color, its greater weight, and its hardness. Microscopically, lack of resin canals and presence of helical thickenings in all tracheids are diagnostic for this wood.

MICROSCOPIC FEATURES—SOFTWOODS

There may appear to be some repetition in the description of anatomical features used in identifying softwoods, but again it is due to the overlap of scale from gross to hand lens to light microscope level. Appropriate illustrations may appear with the macroscopic features or with the microscopic features depending on the relative emphasis being placed on overlapping structural evidence.

Normal and Traumatic Resin Canals

Normal resin canals are a constant feature of the wood of *Pinus, Picea, Larix,* and *Pseudotsuga.* In these genera they run longitudinally and transversely, the latter in the wood rays. Longitudinal and transverse resin canals are in communication.

Normal resin canals have disappeared in *Tsuga* and *Abies* of the Pinaceae, and from the wood of the other six families of the Coniferales. Longitudinal traumatic (wound) canals occur occasionally in native coniferous woods, not only in those devoid of normal canals but also in those having normal canals. In such cases, their presence probably is due to reversion, a "going back" to an ancestral condition, occasioned by wounding. In native conifers, the presence of horizontal resin canals (in fusiform rays) indicates that the wood contains normal resin canals as well.

Figures 42 and 43 illustrate the presence or absence of normal resin canals and the nature of the horizontal resin canals.

Ray Tracheids

Ray tracheids occur as normal structures in the woods of *Pinus, Picea, Pseudotsuga, Larix,* and *Tsuga* of the Pinaceae and in *Chamaecyparis nootkatensis.* These cells are confined to one or a few rows on the upper and lower margins of the rays in *Picea, Larix, Pseudotsuga,* and *Tsuga.* Ray tracheids are most abundant in *Pinus* and in that section of the genus which comprises the hard pines. The low rays of hard pines occasionally consist wholly of ray tracheids, as in *Chamaecyparis nootkatensis,* a species in which some rays are composed exclusively of ray tracheids while others contain only ray parenchyma cells. Also in *Pinus,* the ray tracheids not only form one or more rows on the margin of the rays, but frequently they are found in the body of the ray as well. Ray tracheids occur sporadically in the rays of some other coniferous genera and species but usually are quite limited in occurrence, possibly as a result of injury.

Ray tracheids are dentate (reticulate) in hard pines, nondentate in the soft pines and in other genera where they occur. Very shallow dentations may be found in *Larix* and *Picea,* but these are usually quite indistinct.

Photomicrographs of both types of ray tracheids and some of the patterns of distribution are included as Figure 44.

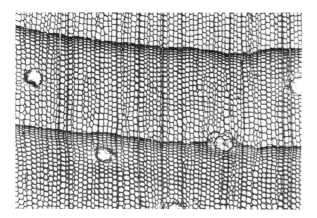

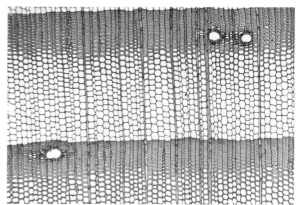

a. Normal resin canals present and abundant

Pinus strobus, 30X

Eastern white pine

Other examples:
Pinus spp.
Picea spp.

b. Normal resin canals present but sporadic and primarily in latewood

Pseudotsuga menziesii, 28X

Douglas-fir

Other example:
Larix spp.

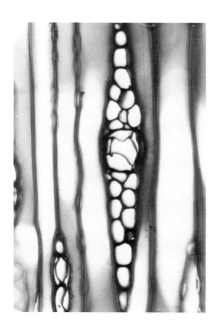

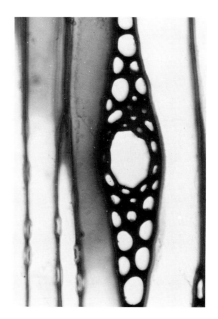

c. Fusiform ray with resin canal; epithelial cells thin-walled

Pinus banksiana, 290X

Jack pine

Other example:
Pinus spp.

d. Fusiform ray with resin canal; epithelial cells thick-walled

Picea sitchensis, 290X

Sitka spruce

Other examples:
Picea spp.
Larix spp.
Pseudotsuga spp.

Figure 42. Normal resin canals present (cross-section) (a) and (b); normal resin canals present in tangential section (in fusiform rays) (c) and (d).

a. Normal resin canals absent (cross-section)

Thuja occidentalis, 28X

Northern white cedar

Other examples:
All except *Pinus spp.,
Larix spp., Picea spp.,* and
Pseudotsuga spp.

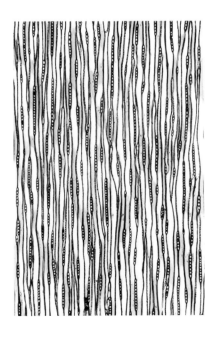

b. Normal resin canals absent (tangential section)

Taxodium distichum, 32.5X

Baldcypress

Other examples:
As for 43a

Figure 43. Examples of softwoods without normal resin canals.

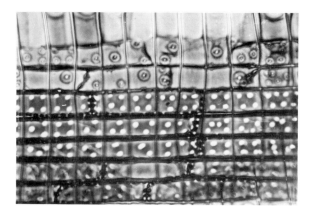

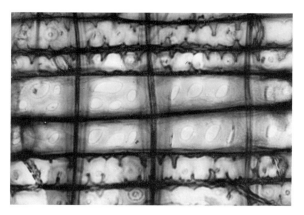

a. Ray tracheids present, usually marginal, combined with ray parenchyma

Picea rubens, 290X

Red spruce

Other examples:
Larix spp.,
Tsuga spp.,
Pseudotsuga spp.

b. Ray tracheids present, dentate, marginal, and interspersed, combined with ray parenchyma

Pinus palustris, 440X

Longleaf pine

Other examples:
Pinus spp. (hard pines)

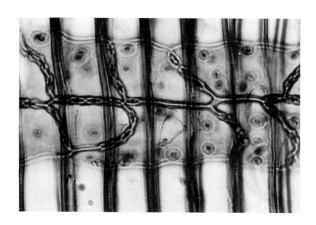

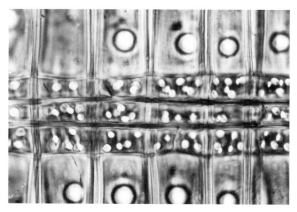

c. Ray tracheids present, separate from ray parenchyma and constituting low rays

Chamaecyparis nootkatensis, 460X

Alaska-cedar

Other examples:
none

d. Ray tracheids normally absent (rays all ray parenchyma)

Thuja plicata, 285X

Western red cedar

Other examples:
Abies, Taxodium, Sequoia,
Juniperus, Libocedrus, and
Taxus spp.

Figure 44. Occurrence and appearance of ray tracheids in softwoods.

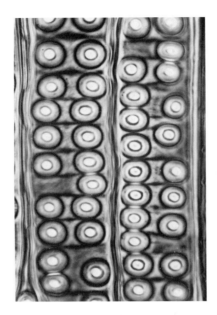
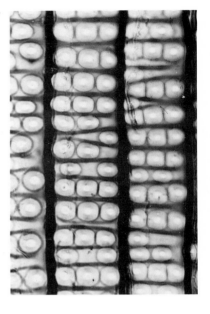

. Radial intertracheid pitting in
ngle rows

inus strobus, 290X

astern white pine

)ther examples: Variable,
ependent upon texture.

b. Radial intertracheid pitting in
paired rows

Larix occidentalis, 500X

Western larch

Other examples: Variable,
dependent upon texture.

c. Radial intertracheid pitting in
multiseriate rows

Taxodium distichum, 290X

Other examples:
Sequoia sempervirens;
Picea sitchensis

Figure 45. Radial intertracheid pitting in softwoods.

Intertracheid Pitting

The bordered pits on the radial walls of the longitudinal tracheids tend to be in one longitudinal row; however, in coarser-textured coniferous woods, the biseriate,
opposite condition may occur along the tracheid. Occasionally three longitudinal rows are found in the earlywood
tracheids of *Taxodium* and *Sequoia* and four rows are visible
in some samples of *Taxodium*. This feature is erratic and
should be used only as a guide. Four consecutive horizontal
rows of the indicated category along the tracheid should be
present to be classified as a positive feature. Figure 45 shows
examples of each of the first three categories of radial wall
pitting.

Crassulae

These structures, also known as Bars of Sanio, are of no diagnostic significance as they occur in all coniferous woods except those from the family Araucariaceae. They are lacking in this instance because crassulae result from the optical density of the cell wall material above and below intertracheid pitting on the radial walls of the tracheids and appear as dark bars. In the Araucariaceae, in contrast to the examples given in the previous section, the bordered pits are staggered rather than occurring in horizontal rows.

Tangential Intertracheid Pitting

Most of the bordered pits in tracheids occur on the radial walls. However, there is some tangential pitting, and when it is present it usually is restricted to the last few rows of latewood tracheids and to the innermost wall of the first row of earlywood tracheids. Pitting has also been noted at the ends of earlywood cells on the tangential surface. It is probable that tangential pitting is of no consequence in separating woods by species or genus. To see the difference in cases where tangential pitting is present or absent, refer to Figure 46.

Parenchyma

Three kinds of parenchyma may be found in coniferous wood: (1) longitudinal (axial) parenchyma; (2) epithelial parenchyma (associated with resin canals); (3) ray parenchyma, which is always present.

Longitudinal parenchyma is wanting in *Pinus* and in the stem wood of *Picea*. It may or may not be present in *Pseudotsuga, Larix, Tsuga*, and *Abies*. When present in the first three genera it is confined to the outer face of the latewood. The same holds true for most species of *Abies*. Of

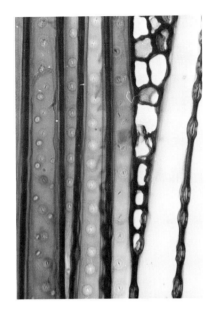 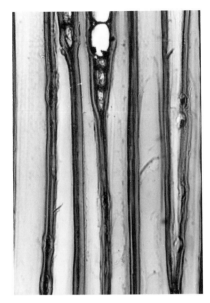

a. Tangential intertracheid pitting
present in last-formed latewood

Pinus strobus, 300X

Eastern white pine

Other examples:
Soft pines

b. Tangential intertracheid pitting
usually absent

Pinus echinata, 310X

Shortleaf pine

Other examples:
Hard pines

Figure 46. Tangential intertracheid pitting in softwoods.

course there may be epithelial parenchyma oriented axially
in those woods having resin canals.

Longitudinal parenchyma is more or less abundant in
the body of the growth ring in *Taxodium, Sequoia, Chamaecyparis, Thuja, Libocedrus, Juniperus,* and *Cupressus.* If
absent from some rings, it occurs in others. There is no
longitudinal parenchyma in *Taxus.*

The appearance of parenchyma in microscope sections can be judged from Figure 47. Scanning micrographs
such as Figure 48 reveal the nature of parenchyma cells in
relation to adjacent prosenchyma.

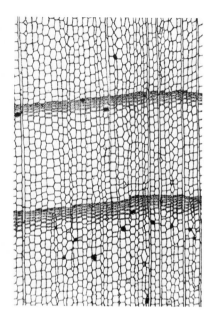

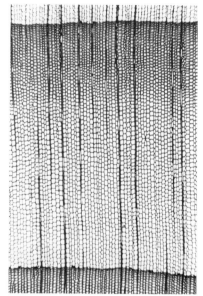

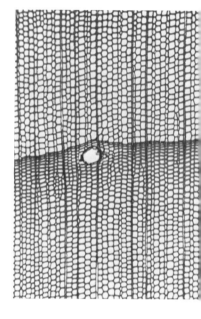

a. Longitudinal (axial parenchyma) present in body of some or of all rings

Sequoia sempervirens, 28X

Redwood

Other examples:
Taxodium distichum;
Chamaecyparis spp.;
Thuja spp.;
Juniperus sp.

b. Longitudinal (axial) parenchyma marginal or absent from many rings

Tsuga heterophylla, 28X

Western hemlock

Other examples:
Abies spp;
Larix spp;
Pseudotsuga menziesii

c. Longitudinal (axial) parenchyma absent or extremely rare

Pinus banksiana, 31X

Jack pine

Other examples:
Picea spp.;
Taxus spp.

Figure 47. Occurrence and arrangement of longitudinal parenchyma in softwoods as viewed on the transverse surface.

Cross Field Pitting

If one examines a microscope section of coniferous wood, the translucency of the cell walls allows the viewing of cell-to-cell relationships, provided that the section is in the thickness range of 10 to 15 micrometers. A radial section invariably reveals ray cells as they cross longitudinal tracheids perpendicularly. The area outlined by the cell walls of such a longitudinal cell and those of the ray cell crossing it is termed a "cross field." The nature of the pit pairs found within a cross field is helpful evidence in identifying many softwoods. The pit pairs are semi-bordered; that is, they consist of a simple pit in the ray parenchyma wall and a bordered pit in the tracheid wall. Distinct shapes characterize various genera and species.

Windowlike pit pairs characterize the soft pines and *Pinus resinosa* and *Pinus sylvestris* of the hard pines. Pinoid pit pairs are found in the remaining native commercial hard pines. In *Picea*, *Larix*, and *Pseudotsuga*, the cross field pit pairs are of the piceoid type. Taxodioid pit pairs occur in *Sequoia*, *Abies*, and *Thuja*. The pit pairs of *Taxodium* are somewhat of an anomaly since they may be taxodioid or cupressoid. Cupressaceous woods, *Thuja* excepted, and *Tsuga* have cupressoid pit pairs. These various pit pair shapes are illustrated in photomicrographs in Figure 49.

Texture

The best measure of texture in coniferous woods is the tangential diameter of the average tracheid. There is a broad range of texture in softwoods. Redwood and baldcypress are the coarsest-textured with diameters up to 80 micrometers. Western yew and eastern red cedar are at the other end of the scale with tracheid diameters in the order of 15 to 20 micrometers.

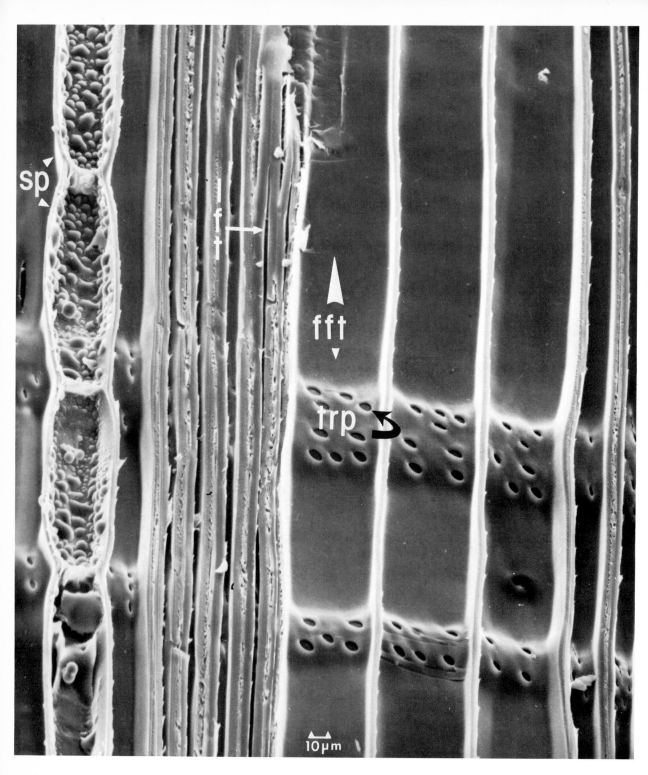

Figure 48a. Scanning electron micrograph of the radial surface of redwood, *Sequoia sempervirens*, showing longitudinal strand parenchyma (sp) adjacent to the last-formed tracheids in one growth ring. The pitted ray parenchyma cells are located under the two horizontal bands which appear as bulges in the tracheid. The tracheid-to-ray pitting (trp) would appear as taxodioid pitting in a cross-field when viewed with a light microscope. The first-formed tracheid of a growth increment is indicated as (fft).

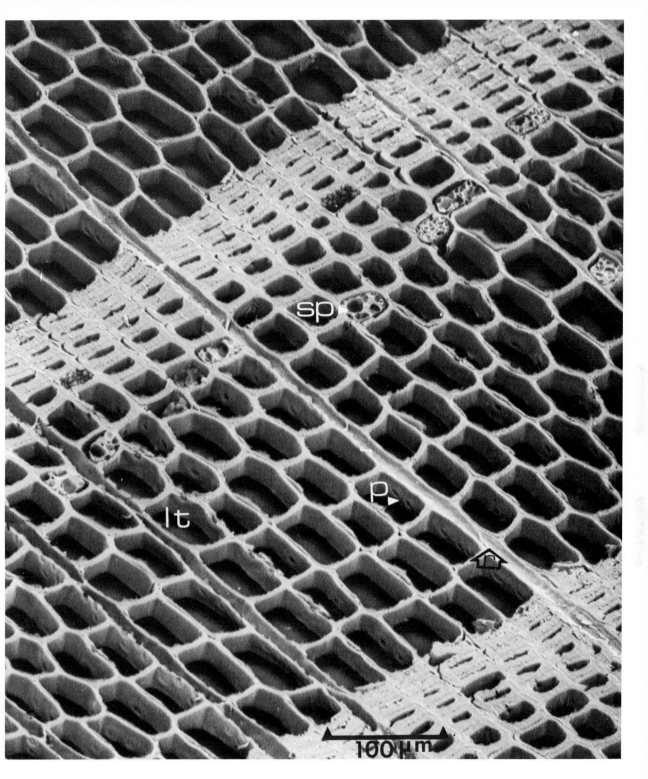

Figure 48b. Scanning electron micrograph of the cross-sectional surface of redwood, *Sequoia sempervirens*, showing longitudinal strand parenchyma (sp), with cell contents, scattered among longitudinal tracheids (lt). Note the ray structure (r) and the pitting between ray parenchyma cells and longitudinal tracheids at arrow (p).

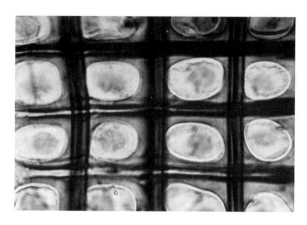

a. Cross field pitting window-like (fenestriform)

Pinus strobus, 675X

Eastern white pine

Other examples:
Pinus monticola
Pinus resinosa

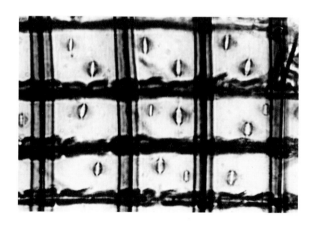

b. Cross field pitting pinoid

Pinus ponderosa, 575X

Ponderosa pine

Other examples:
Pinus contorta;
Southern yellow pines

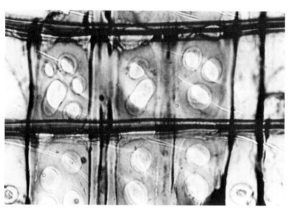

c. Cross field pitting piceoid

Picea sitchensis, 750X

Sitka spruce

Other examples:
Larix laricina;
Picea spp.

Figure 49

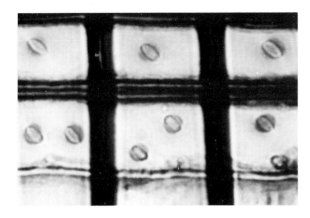

d. Cross field pitting cupressoid
Libocedrus decurrens, 1125X
Incense cedar
Other examples:
Chamaecyparis spp.;
Juniperus spp.

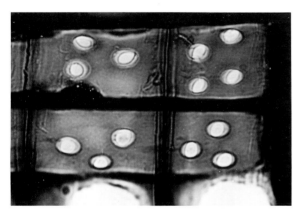

e. Cross field pitting taxodioid
Sequoia sempervirens, 650X
Redwood
Other examples:
Thuja spp.;
Abies spp.

Figure 49. Cross field pitting between ray parenchyma cells and longitudinal tracheids in conifers as viewed in radial section.

Helical (Spiral) Thickenings

The inner walls of tracheids, both longitudinal and ray, may be sculptured or decorated with helical (spiral) thickenings. These ropelike strands are found in *Pseudotsuga*, *Taxus*, and *Torreya* species. Usually the latewood tracheids of *Pseudotsuga* are lacking helical thickenings.

The helices may occur very sporadically in the latewood of *Larix* and the southern hard pines. Seasoning checks in the thick-walled latewood tracheids of *Pinus*, *Larix*, and others should not be confused with helical thickenings, nor should the gaps in the cell walls of compression wood tracheids. The checking is a real opening between cellulose microfibrils, while the thickening is the addition of material to the secondary wall. Figures 50a and 14a illustrate the difference as viewed with the light microscope and the scanning electron microscope.

Ray Parenchyma Sculpturing

The cell walls of ray parenchyma may be sculptured and thus provide consistent diagnostic evidence for separating some of the genera and species. This feature is related primarily to cell wall thickness and resultant appearance when pitted. For example, the end walls may appear "nodular" if the walls there are relatively thick and pitted. Species of *Tsuga*, *Abies*, *Picea*, as well as *Libocedrus decurrens* have such nodular end walls. On the other hand these end walls are smooth in species of *Thuja*, in *Sequoia sempervirens*, and also in *Taxodium distichum* ray parenchyma cells. Figures 51a and 51b illustrate these features.

The transverse walls (upper and lower horizontal walls) of ray parenchyma may be well pitted. Species of *Larix*, *Abies*, and *Tsuga* fall into this category. The opposite condition applies to *Sequoia sempervirens* and *Taxodium distichum* which have smooth transverse walls. Compare Figures 51c and 51d for these structures.

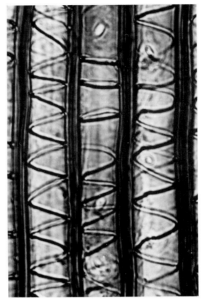

a. Spiral (helical) checks in softwood tracheids due to seasoning or to the presence of compression wood as in this example

Pseudotsuga menziesii, 625X

Douglas-fir

Other examples:
Checks due to these causes have been found in virtually all coniferous species

b. Spiral (helical) thickening in softwood tracheids

Taxus brevifolia, 700X

Pacific yew

Other example:
Pseudotsuga spp.

Figure 50. Helical thickenings in longitudinal tracheids contrasted with checking in the cell walls.

Finally there is a structure known as an "indenture" on the transverse walls of ray parenchyma in *Thuja occidentalis.* This depression in the wall looks much like a pit, but it is simply a sculptured area near the ends of the cells. See Figure 51e for a photomicrograph of this feature.

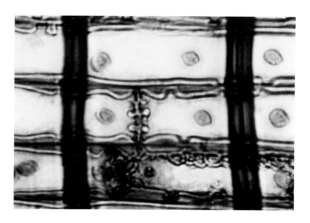

a. End (vertical) walls of ray parenchyma nodular

Abies balsamea, 1040X

Balsam fir

Other examples:
Abies spp.;
Picea spp.

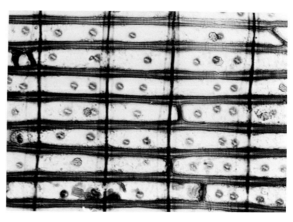

b. End (vertical) walls of ray parenchyma smooth

Taxodium distichum, 312X

Baldcypress

Other examples:
Thuja spp.;
Sequoia sp.

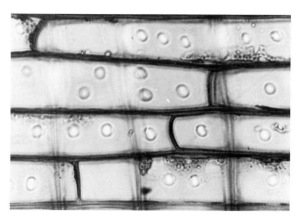

c. Transverse (horizontal) walls of ray cells smooth

Sequoia sempervirens, 410X

Redwood

Other example:
Taxodium spp.

Figure 51. Sculpturing of ray parenchyma cell walls in softwoods.

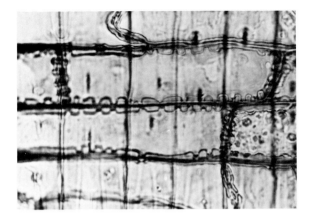

d. Transverse (horizontal) walls of ray cells pitted
Larix occidentalis, 625X
Western larch
Other examples:
Picea spp.;
Tsuga spp.;
Larix spp.

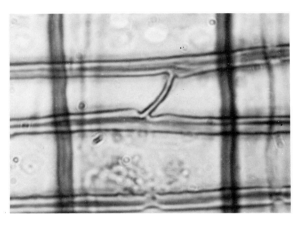

e. Indentures present on transverse walls
of ray cells (at junction
of end wall)
Thuja plicata, 1100X
Western red cedar
Other examples:
Taxodium spp.;
Juniperus spp.

Figure 51 (continued).

Longitudinal Parenchyma Sculpturing

The axially oriented parenchyma discussed earlier has end walls with characteristics very similar to the ray parenchyma. The end walls of these longitudinal elements are best observed in a tangential section where the wall would appear as a horizontal smooth membrane in woods such as

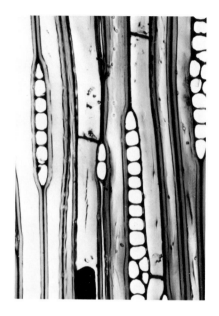 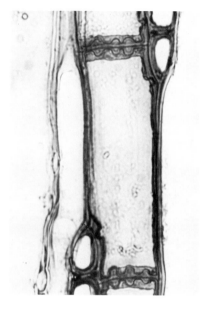

a. End (horizontal) walls smooth
Sequoia sempervirens, 40X
Redwood
Other example:
Chamaecyparis thyoides

b. End (horizontal) walls nodular
Taxodium distichum, 500X
Baldcypress
Other example:
Libocedrus decurrens

Figure 52. Nature of the end walls of longitudinal (axial) parenchyma in softwoods.

Sequoia sempervirens. In *Taxodium distichum* and *Libocedrus decurrens* the wall is nodular. Figure 52 contrasts these features clearly.

Strand Tracheids

Strand tracheids are found in softwoods occasionally. They appear in the vicinity of resin canals or contiguous to longitudinal parenchyma. They have the shape of parenchyma cells but are tracheid-like in nature, with bordered pits. Parenchyma cells have simple pits.

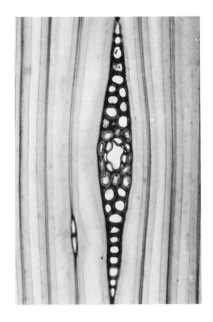

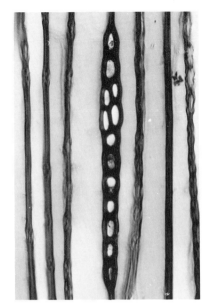

a. Fusiform rays (rays with resin canals)
Pseudotsuga menziesii, 200X
Douglas-fir
Other examples:
Picea spp.;
Larix spp.

b. Biseriate rays (rarely multiseriate)
Libocedrus decurrens, 375X
Incense-cedar
Other examples:
Sequoia sempervirens;
Taxodium distichum

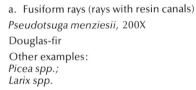

Figure 53. Fusiform rays (with resin canals) and biseriate rays of conifers, as viewed in tangential section.

Ray Size (Width and Height)

Softwoods have narrow rays except where transverse canals are present. Then the ray becomes fusiform in the tangential view as shown in Figure 53a. In woods containing fusiform rays, the narrow rays far outnumber fusiform rays. Fusiform rays are found only in species of *Pinus, Picea, Larix,* and in *Pseudotsuga menziesii.*

Narrow rays in coniferous woods prevailingly are uniseriate but vary greatly in height. The cedars as a group tend to have low rays while the true firs (*Abies*) have high rays. In some woods such as redwood and incense cedar, there is more or less of a tendency toward the biseriate condition illustrated in Figure 53b.

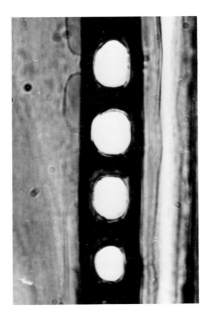 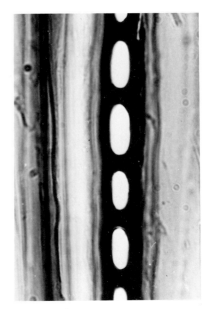

a. Isodiametric ray cells
Picea sitchensis, 1000X
Sitka spruce
Other examples:
Sequoia sempervirens;
Taxodium distichum

b. Elongated (oval) ray cells
Picea rubens, 1000X
Red spruce
Other examples:
Larix spp.

Figure 54. Variation in ray cell shape in conifers.

Ray Parenchyma Shape (Tangential View)

It is possible to separate the wood of eastern spruces from that of Sitka spruce on the basis of the shape of the ray parenchyma cells as viewed on a tangential section. Sitka spruce has cells that appear isodiametric in shape while those of the eastern spruces are elongated (oval). Redwood ray cells would appear much like the Sitka spruce. However, because of other obvious characteristics, these two woods are not likely to be confused. Refer to Figure 54 for photomicrographs illustrating these ray parenchyma shapes.

Trabeculae

Sometimes one will find rodlike structures traversing tracheid lumens from one tangential wall to another. When they are present, they usually extend across several tracheids in a radial direction, and they may appear in more than one row. They are believed to be traceable to cambial fungi, and because of their random and sporadic occurrence, they are of no diagnostic significance. In Figure 55, a scanning electron micrograph of the wood of Douglas-fir, there is a good example of a trabecula.

Crystals

Crystals have been noted in the ray parenchyma cells of many of the softwoods. Rhomboidal and rectangular crystals are rather common in some species of *Abies*. Sometimes this may be used as a diagnostic guide. In a photomicrograph these crystals appear as shown in Figure 56. With the scanning electron microscope (SEM) and energy-dispersive x-ray analysis (EDXA), it is now possible to determine something of the chemical nature of such crystals. For a discussion of this technique, refer to the section on crystals in hardwoods and Figure 39.

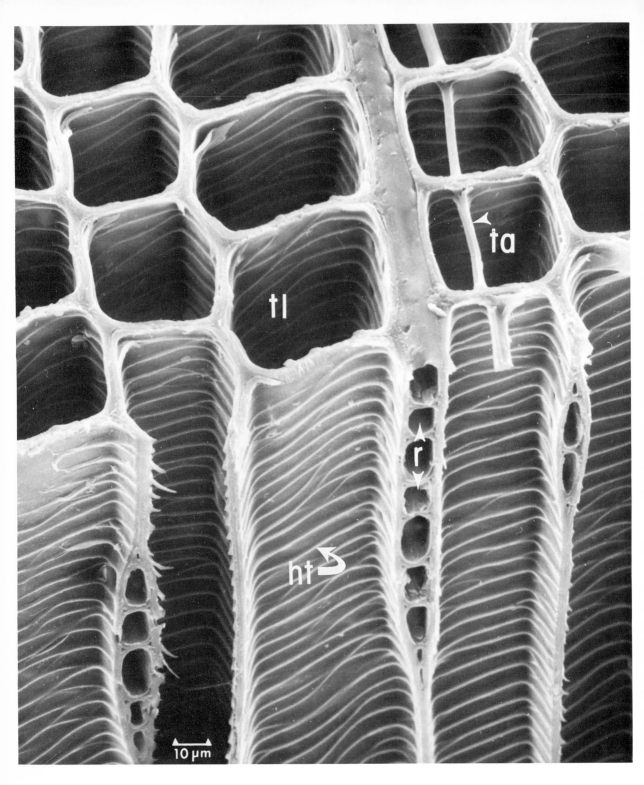

Figure 55. Scanning electron micrograph of Douglas-fir wood with the rod-like trabecula (ta) traversing the tracheid lumens (tl) in a radial direction. Helical thickenings (ht) line the tracheid walls. Several rays (r) can be seen on the tangential surface, and one is visible on both tangential and transverse surfaces.

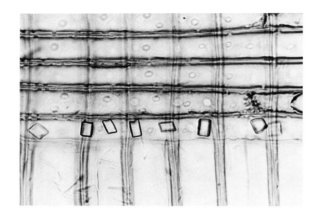

Abies concolor, 310X
White fir
Rare in other species.

Figure 56. Crystals in ray parenchyma of conifers.

Intercellular Spaces

In most softwoods, there is little space found between cells when a cross-section is examined with a light microscope. The cells are rather tightly packed as a result of growth pressures. However, in *Juniperus virginiana* it is possible to find intercellular spaces that are characteristic in normal wood. Emphasis is placed on this point because compression wood (coniferous reaction wood) is characterized by rounded tracheid cross-sections and such intercellular spaces. This was shown in Figure 14a. Note that such tracheids have other features as well: gaps in the secondary wall and fewer cell wall layers. There are also variations in chemical composition such as higher lignin content.

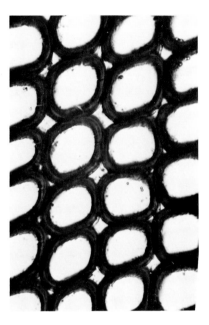 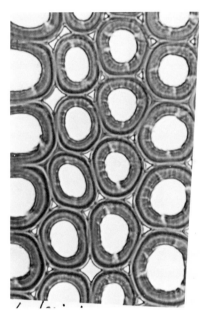

a. Intercellular spaces normal
Juniperus virginiana, 625X
Eastern red cedar
Other examples:
None

b. Intercellular spaces due to
presence of compression wood
Larix laricina, 625X
Eastern larch
Other examples:
May occur in any conifer

Figure 57. Intercellular spaces normal (a) and due to the presence of compressed wood (b).

Figure 57a illustrates intercellular spaces in normal eastern redcedar, while Figure 57b is a photomicrograph of compression wood in eastern larch.

3

Keys for the Identification of Hardwoods and Softwoods

IDENTIFICATION KEYS

The literature contains an abundance of keys for the identification of wood. Some are good; some are fair; none are completely satisfactory to the user. The difficulty of communication between the developer and the user of keys and the variability of separate pieces of wood of the same species make most keys cumbersome and laborious to use. Often, by the time a user has developed facility with a key, he has constructed a "key of the mind" which will be used more frequently than the written key.

Keys are relatively easy to construct and may be quite useful for a limited number of species or for a restricted region. As the number of species increases and/or the importance of exact separation grows, the key becomes more and more difficult to construct.

Of course, woods not included in the key cannot be identified. It is suggested that the user modify the keys for his purposes or obtain a key already developed for the woods in which he is interested.

One of the best methods for accurate identification involves the use of card-sorting keys. Each species is represented by a card which is edge-punched with the appropriate features or characters. This system allows the user to concentrate on unusual or unique features immediately without tracking laboriously through a dichotomous key of the type used in this manual. For the preparation of card keys, the reader is referred to the following sources which are cited in the reference list: (1) *The Identification of Coniferous Woods by Their Microscopic Structure,* by E. W. J. Phillips, and (2) *Identification of Hardwoods—A Lens Key,* which is a Forest Products Research Bulletin published in England.

The value of comparing unknown samples with standard or known materials cannot be overemphasized. It follows that one should develop a collection of samples that have been authenticated and that these be used as diagnostic skills are improved. The suggestions offered in Appendix D may prove quite useful in starting such a collection.

A few guidelines will make the use of the keys that follow more effective. Dichotomous keys, the type used in this manual, are based on paired choices of features. The user selects the description that more nearly fits the sample under consideration and follows the indicated number to the next pair of choices. The rejected features may reappear later due to variation or overlapping of structural evidence.

As a first step it is convenient to separate woods into the two broad groups, softwoods and hardwoods, before any attempt is made at identification by species. The softwoods lack vessels, have fine rays (uniseriate except when resin canals are present), and show radial alignment of cells (tracheids) on the cross-section. The hardwoods contain vessels and, with few exceptions, possess multiseriate rays and lack radial alignment of cells on the cross-section. Hardwoods also are more complex in that they have more types of elements and more patterns of tissue arrangement.

The features used in these keys are gross (visible with the unaided eye) or hand lens features (visible with a hand lens of 5X to 10X), to the extent possible. Softwoods require light microscope examination for accurate identification to species in many instances. Should the user desire additional microscopic features on which to base a diagnosis, the section "Features Useful for Wood Identification" provides illustrated descriptions of the important structural characteristics. Additionally, reference may be made to a more detailed source, such as *Textbook of Wood Technology,* Vol. I, by Panshin and de Zeeuw.

KEY TO SOFTWOODS

1. Wood with resin canals. [Examine for fusiform (wide) rays on cross section and resin canal evidence on both cross-section and tangential surface] 2

1. Wood without resin canals 13

   2. Wood with abrupt transition 3

   2. Wood with gradual or semi-gradual transition 5

3. Wood with strong resinous odor, resin canals large and somewhat uniformly distributed, ray tracheids dentate . . . . *Pinus* spp.
                   Southern yellow pines, Western yellow pine

3. Wood lacking strong resinous odor. A characteristic distinct odor may be present 4

   4. Wood with distinctive odor, resin canals mostly in latewood in tangential rows of 2-several. Longitudinal tracheids with spiral (helical) thickenings in earlywood . . . . *Pseudotsuga* spp.
                             Douglas-fir

   4. Wood with little or no scent, earlywood tracheids without helical thickenings . . . . *Larix* spp.
                             Larch

5. Wood with resinous odor, resin canals relatively abundant and conspicuous. Cross field pitting window-like to pinoid 6

5. Wood lacking resinous odor, resin canals sporadic, frequently aggregated. Cross field pitting piceoid, cupressoid 7

   6. Transition of growth ring gradual, cross field pitting window-like, ray tracheids non-dentate (Soft pines) . . . 8

   6. Transition of growth ring semi-abrupt, cross field pitting pinoid, ray tracheids dentate 10

7. Transition of growth ring gradual, woods lustrous, yellowish-white, cross field pitting piceoid to cupressoid . . . . *Picea* spp.
                             Spruces

7. Transition of growth ring semi-abrupt, wood with purplish cast, texture coarse, cross field pitting piceoid . . . . *Picea sitchensis*
                             Sitka spruce

8. Window-like pitting rectangular in earlywood.
Usually one pit to a cross field . . . . *Pinus strobus*
Eastern white pine

8. Window-like pitting rhomboidal and oval. Usually
more than one pit per cross field 9

9. Cross field pitting rhomboidal, wood
of medium texture . . . . *Pinus monticola*
Western white pine

9. Cross field pitting oval (port holes),
coarse textured . . . . *Pinus lambertiana*
Sugar pine

10. Cross field pitting pinoid; ray tracheids conspicuously
dentate 11

10. Cross field pitting window-like in earlywood. Usually,
one pit per cross field. Ray tracheids rather shallowly
dentate 12

11. Latewood bands distinct, resin canals
medium in size . . . . *Pinus ponderosa*
Ponderosa pine

11. Latewood bands indistinct and narrow; resin canals small.
Wood frequently with dimpling on
tangential surface . . . . *Pinus contorta*
Lodgepole pine

12. Window-like pits horizontally elongated. Frequently
twice as long as high. Resin canals small and inconspicuous; confined for the most part to
the middle and latewood
portion of the ring . . . . *Pinus resinosa*
Red pine

12. Window-like pits
rectangular to square . . . . *Pinus sylvestris**
Scots pine

13. Wood with distinct, fragrant or spicy odor. Longitudinal
parenchyma often abundant. Ray tracheids lacking
or in homogeneous rays (cedars) 14

13. Wood without distinct odor; occasionally with a
disagreeable odor 20

*Although an exotic, scots pine has been planted extensively in the northeastern United States. Also, it is the most important softwood of Europe. It has not been included in Table 1.

14. Wood yellowish, odor spicy, resembling that of
  . potato peelings, some low rays consisting entirely
     of ray tracheids .... *Chamaecyparis nootkatensis*
                                          Alaska cedar

14. Wood in varying shades of red, brown, tan, or
     straw yellow 15

15. Wood reddish, with fine texture and
    uniform consistency .... *Juniperus virginiana*
                                          Eastern red cedar

15. Wood in shades of brown, tan, or straw yellow 16

16. Transition of growth ring abrupt, odor faintly
    chocolate and sweetish. Wood easily
    split along grain .... *Thuja plicata*
                                          Western red cedar

16. Transition of growth ring gradual 17

17. Wood with ginger-like odor.
    Zonate parenchyma visible
    on moist cross section .... *Chamaecyparis lawsoniana*
                                          Port Orford cedar

17. Wood with spicy odor, not ginger-like 18

18. Wood with flesh-color tint, spicy, zonate parenchyma
    visible on moist cross section
       .... *Chamaecyparis thyoides*
                                  Southern white cedar

18. Wood brown, tan, or straw yellow 19

19. Wood brownish, even textured,
    odor like that of pencil shavings .... *Libocedrus decurrens*
                                          Incense cedar

19. Wood straw yellow or tan, soft and
    light. Cross field pitting taxodioid ...... *Thuja occidentalis*
                                  Northern white cedar

20. Wood reddish, very fine textured, hard, and heavy.
    Longitudinal parenchyma absent.
    Helical thickenings present
    in all tracheids .... *Taxus brevifolia*
                                          Pacific yew

20. Wood in varying shades of red, brown,
    or yellow, coarse to medium textured, helical
    thickenings absent 21

21. Wood reddish, lacking distinct odor, coarse textured,
    splitting easily along the grain. Beaded parenchyma
    visible with lens on split surface.
    Ray tracheids lacking . . . . *Sequoia sempervirens*
                                                    Redwood
21. Wood in shades of brown or yellow, rarely with reddish
    color 22

    22. Wood coarse textured, usually with rancid odor and
    oily appearance. Beaded parenchyma visible on split
    surface. Yellowish to brown
    occasionally with reddish cast.
    Ray tracheids absent . . . . *Taxodium distichum*
                                                Baldcypress
    22. Wood medium textured, odorless, sometimes with un-
    usual odor, parenchyma not visible, or absent 23

23. Wood semi-abrupt in transition, dry to touch, light tan.
    Ray tracheids present as narrow or low,
    indistinct marginal rows. Cross field pitting
    cupressoid to piceoid . . . . *Tsuga* spp.
                                                                Hemlocks
23. Wood gradual to semi-gradual in transition, yellowish
    white to white. Ray tracheids absent. Cross field pitting
    taxodioid. Wood sometimes with unusual
    odor, pleasant or malodorous . . . . *Abies* spp.
                                                                True firs

KEY TO HARDWOODS

Ring- and Semi-Ring-Porous Woods

1. Wood ring-porous; earlywood pores obviously larger than
   those in the latewood. Earlywood pores sometimes restricted to a single, continuous, or interrupted row 2
1. Wood semi-ring-porous. Earlywood pores not obviously
   larger than adjacent latewood pores of same ring. Occasionally, a single row of slightly larger pores may be pres-
   ent at beginning of ring 28

2. Wood with broad, oak-type rays 3

2. Wood lacking broad, oak-type rays 4

3. Latewood pores rounded, easily visible with
hand lens, grouped and forming an
oblique pattern across the ring .... *Quercus* spp.
                                                    Red oaks

3. Latewood pores angular, crowded, and thin-walled. Difficult to see with hand lens; grouped and forming
an oblique pattern across the ring .... *Quercus* spp.
                                                    White oaks

4. Apotracheal banded parenchyma present; visible on
wetted surface in latewood with hand lens 5

4. Apotracheal banded parenchyma absent or not visible
with hand lens 8

5. Rays storied, forming ripple marks on the tangential surface. Apotracheal banded parenchyma
in fine lines, forming a net-like pattern
with the rays .... *Diospyros virginiana*
                                                    Persimmon

5. Rays unstoried, apotracheal parenchyma
forming a ladder-like pattern with the rays, sometimes
distinct and restricted to outer portion of ring 6

6. Apotracheal parenchyma consistent and extending
to earlywood zone. Wood tan or
reddish brown .... *Carya* spp.
                                                    True hickories

6. Apotracheal parenchyma sporadic and indistinct;
restricted to outer margin of latewood 7

7. Heartwood chocolate- to purplish-brown;
moderately hard (resistant to thumbnail
indentation) .... *Juglans nigra*
                                                    Black walnut

7. Heartwood pale brown, frequently with a
flesh tint. Wood soft (easily dented with
thumbnail) .... *Juglans cinerea*
                                                    Butternut

8. Latewood pores small, numerous; clustered in groups
or patches (flame-shaped) obliquely radial to growth
ring. Rays very fine (uniseriate) and indistinct 9

8. Latewood pores not as above. Rays multiseriate;
sometimes indistinct to eye 10

9. Earlywood pores in several rows; pores large (300μm). Wood grayish-brown to brown . . . . *Castanea dentata*
American chestnut

9. Earlywood pores in a single row; wood light brown, occasionally pinkish . . . . *Castanopsis chrysophylla*
Golden chinkapin

    10. Latewood pores in ulmiform pattern forming wavy, tangential bands that are more or less continuous 11

    10. Latewood pores not in ulmiform pattern 18

11. Earlywood pores restricted to a single row 12

11. Earlywood pores in several rows, at least in part 13

    12. Earlywood pores in a continuous, uninterrupted row . . . . *Ulmus americana*
American elm

    12. Earlywood pores in a discontinuous, interrupted row; wood hard and heavy . . . . *Ulmus* spp.
Cork elm, winged elm

13. Rays storied, forming ripple marks on the tangential surface. Heartwood dull brown . . . . *Cercis canadensis*
Redbud

13. Wood without storied rays 14

    14. Heartwood pores completely occluded with tyloses; greenish to dark brown. Wood very hard and heavy 15

    14. Heartwood pores not completely occluded with tyloses sometimes numerous 16

15. Earlywood pores clearly outlined on smooth cross section. Vestures present in intervessel pitting . . . . *Robinia pseudoacacia*
Black locust

15. Earlywood pores indistinct in outline on smooth cross section. Water extract of chips yellowish . . . . *Maclura pomifera*
Osage orange

16. Heartwood in varying shades of brown or
golden brown. Tyloses numerous. Latewood pores
with tendency to form nests. Rays
distinct to unaided eye .... *Morus rubra*
Mulberry

16. Heartwood greenish yellow or reddish. Tyloses scattered. Latewood pores merging into background. Rays
barely visible to the unaided eye 17

17. Heartwood reddish. Rays indistinct to the eye.
Wood often with disagreeable odor
when wetted .... *Ulmus rubra*
Red elm

17. Heartwood greenish yellow. Rays fairly
distinct to eye. Rows of earlywood pores
variable in number .... *Celtis* spp.
Hackberry

18. Paratracheal parenchyma absent or not evident 19

18. Paratracheal parenchyma present, sometimes
restricted to the outer margin of the ring;
occasionally confluent 20

19. Latewood pores in nestlike groups. Earlywood pores large,
forming several rows. Rays uniform and visible to eye.
Wood usually with distinct
reddish cast .... *Gymnocladus dioicus*
Kentucky coffee tree

19. Latewood pores solitary and in multiples. Earlywood
pores in a ragged, uniseriate row.
Heartwood yellowish-brown
tinged with red .... *Rhamnus caroliniana*
Buckthorn

20. Tyloses lacking in heartwood; reddish gum plugs
occasionally found in vessels 21

20. Tyloses present in heartwood. Rays appearing
uniform in size and spacing 22

21. Heartwood with reddish cast. Pores occasionally
    with gum plugs. Rays appearing
    in two distinct sizes .... *Gleditsia triacanthos*
                                              Honeylocust

21. Wood light brown and dull. Pores appearing thick-walled
    due to encircling parenchyma. Latewood pores
    scattered, not occupying
    one-half of the surface .... *Albizia julibrissin*
                                               Mimosa

    22. Heartwood pores completely occluded with tyloses;
         wood hard and heavy 23

    22. Heartwood pores not completely occluded
         with tyloses 24

23. Earlywood pores clearly outlined on smooth cross section.
    Vestured pitting present
    in vessels .... *Robinia pseudoacacia*
                                       Black locust

23. Earlywood pores indistinct in outline on smooth
    cross section. Water extract of
    small chips yellowish .... *Maclura pomifera*
                                            Osage orange

    24. Rays distinct to the eye. Heartwood
         with distinct, spicy odor .... *Sassafras albidum*
                                                Sassafras

    24. Rays indistinct to the eye. Heartwood odorless or
         with musty odor 25

25. Heartwood with musty odor; wood soft and weak 26

25. Heartwood odorless; wood relatively hard 27

    26. Latewood pores small and indistinct; paratracheal
         parenchyma confluent in extreme outer portion
         of ring but lacking in middle of ring ...... *Catalpa* spp.
                                                    Catalpa

    26. Latewood pores large; paratracheal parenchyma
         frequently confluent in middle of ring
         and connecting pore multiples
         in an echelon pattern .... *Paulownia tomentosa*
                                         Paulownia; Princess-tree

27. Wood grayish brown, generally lustrous. Latewood
pores scattered. Paratracheal parenchyma
confluent in outer margin of ring . . . . . . *Fraxinus americana*
White ash

27. Wood brown. Growth rings usually narrow. Latewood
pores scattered. Paratracheal parenchyma rarely
confluent in outer margin of ring.
Wood non-lustrous . . . . *Fraxinus nigra*
Brown ash

  28. Rays of two distinct sizes, the largest either oak-type
  or aggregate. Latewood pores small, unevenly
  distributed, clustered in
  radially oblique groups . . . . *Lithocarpus densiflorus*
  Tan oak

  28. Rays not of two distinct sizes, sometimes very small
  and not visible to the eye 29

29. Rays extremely fine (uniseriate) and barely visible with a
hand lens. Pores numerous, appearing to occupy over
half of surface 30

29. Rays easily visible with hand lens and/or unaided eye 31

  30. Heartwood whitish to very light brown, soft and
  light. Rays homocellular . . . . *Populus* spp.
  Cottonwoods

  30. Heartwood brownish or reddish brown, soft
  and light. Rays heterocellular . . . . *Salix* spp.
  Willows

31. Earlywood pores arranged in a uniseriate, more or less
continuous row; distinct. Rays visible to the eye 32

31. Earlywood pore zone not distinct. Pores decreasing
gradually in size 34

  32. Paratracheal parenchyma present, encircling pores to
  form a thick wall. Heartwood clear yellow to light
  brown. Tyloses absent. Brownish gum
  plugs sometimes evident in pores . . . . *Cladrastis lutea*
  Yellow wood

  32. Paratracheal parenchyma not evident. Pores
  numerous, solitary, in multiples, and in nests 33

33. Heartwood uniformly reddish brown; rays clearly
visible to eye . . . . *Prunus serotina*
Black cherry

33. Heartwood yellowish brown, frequently tinged with red.
Earlywood pores in a ragged, uniseriate
or mostly uniseriate row . . . . *Rhamnus caroliniana*
Buckthorn

34. Paratracheal parenchyma present, at least in outer
margin of latewood; occasionally confluent.
Wood soft, dull brown with musty odor . . *Catalpa* spp.
Catalpa

34. Parenchyma apotracheal banded or not evident 35

35. Rays storied, forming ripple marks on the tangential
surface; apotracheal parenchyma abundant, appearing as
short, closely spaced lines between rays. Wood (sapwood
is used) creamy white to grayish brown.
Hard and heavy . . . . *Diospyros virginiana*
Persimmon

35. Rays unstoried 36

36. Heartwood purplish brown or chocolate brown;
apotracheal banded parenchyma indistinct
and restricted to outer portion
of growth ring . . . . *Juglans nigra*
Black walnut

36. Heartwood light brown to reddish brown,
apotracheal parenchyma distinct at least in outer
portion of ring 37

37. Heartwood light brown to reddish brown, hard and
heavy. Apotracheal banded parenchyma abundant and
distinct as horizontal lines between
the rays (ladder-like) . . . . *Carya* spp.
Pecan hickories

37. Heartwood light brown, frequently with a flesh tint. Wood
light and soft (easily dented with thumbnail). Apotracheal
banded parenchyma restricted to outer
portion of ring . . . . *Juglans cinerea*
Butternut

Diffuse-Porous Woods

1. Rays consisting of two distinct sizes (x), the larger plainly
    visible to the eye and wider than the largest pores 2
1. Rays not consisting of two distinct sizes (x), conspicuous to
    fine and not visible to the eye 7

  2. Large rays appearing non-uniform in size and irreg-
      ularly spaced 3
  2. Large rays appearing uniform in size and spacing 5

3. Large rays very erratic in distribution, frequently lacking in
    local areas; when present, high and
    conspicuous on tangential surface .... *Alnus rubra*
                                                    Red alder

3. Large rays present, even in small areas 4

  4. Large rays appearing on tangential surface as short
      conspicuous lines, not crowded. Pores numerous, ap-
      pearing to occupy
      one-half or more of surface .... *Fagus grandifolia*
                                            Beech
  4. Large rays inconspicuous on tangential and transverse
      surface. Pores scattered, not
      occupying one-half of surface ... *Carpinus caroliniana*
                                        American hornbeam

5. Pores very small, in radial lines or chains parallel to the
    surface. Large rays inconspicuous, blending
    with background. Wood white .... *Ilex opaca*
                                                Holly

5. Pores small, numerous, and uniformly distributed. Wood
    hard and heavy 6

  6. Sapwood with slight pink or flesh-colored tint.
      Heartwood restricted in size; dark
      brown .... *Cornus florida*
                                        Dogwood
  6. Sapwood creamy white and lustrous. Heart-
      wood restricted in size; reddish brown ..... *Acer* spp.
                                                  Hard maple

7. Pores in groupings or concentrations within the growth
   ring; unevenly distributed   8
7. Pores uniformly distributed throughout growth ring 10

    8. Rays visible to eye; pores minute, in
       radial lines or chains. Wood white . . . . *Ilex opaca*
                                                  Holly
    8. Rays not visible to eye   9

9. Pores with slight tendency toward radial grouping.
   Wood soft; light reddish brown . . . . *Alnus rubra*
                                                       Red alder
9. Pores with tendency to group in radially oblique areas,
   unevenly distributed. Apotracheal banded
   parenchyma usually evident in outer ring
   with hand lens . . . . *Ostrya virginiana*
                                       Ironwood; Hophornbeam

    10. Rays plainly visible to eye 11
    10. Rays indistinct or not visible to eye 14

11. Rays nearly uniform in width 12
11. Rays non-uniform in width, either of two fairly distinct
    sizes or intergrading in width 13

    12. Rays visible on tangential surface as high, closely
        spaced lines; forming a high, distinct
        fleck on the radial surface . . . . . . *Platanus occidentalis*
                                          Sycamore

    12. Rays not visible on tangential surface, forming a low,
        closely spaced fleck on the radial surface.
        Marginal parenchyma evident as a
        distinct, whitish line . . . . *Magnolia* spp.*
                                        Magnolias
                            *Liriodendron tulipifera**
                                    Yellowpoplar

---

*Yellowpoplar and the magnolias cannot be separated with certainty unless microscopic features are used:
    1. *Liriodendron tulipifera*—opposite intervessel pitting; scalariform perfora-
        tions.
    2. *Magnolia acuminata*—scalariform intervessel pitting; scalariform perfora-
        tations in juvenile wood only.
    3. *Magnolia grandiflora*—scalariform intervessel pitting; scalariform perfora-
        tions; thickenings [helical (spiral) thickenings] in
        vessel elements.

13. Rays appearing to be of two distinct widths, visible on tangential surface as short, closely packed lines. Ray fleck low and distinct. Wood hard and heavy, light red to very light tan and lustrous . . . . *Acer* spp.
                                                    Hard maple

13. Rays appearing to intergrade in size from fine to those visible to eye. Ray fleck low and distinct. Wood moderately hard, light brown to very light tan, frequently with grayish cast; non-lustrous . . . . *Acer* spp.
                                                    Soft maple

   14. Wood with spicy odor. Pores scattered and somewhat distant, solitary and in radial multiples, encircled by a whitish sheath of parenchyma . . . . *Umbellularia californica*
                                                    Oregon-myrtle

   14. Wood without spicy odor. Pores numerous and crowded 15

15. Rays fine and close, appearing to occupy one-half or more of surface 16

15. Rays not seeming to occupy one-half or more of surface . . . 18

   16. Wood creamy white to pale yellow, light and soft. Rays constant in size (uniseriate) and often storied . . . . *Aesculus* spp.
                                                    Buckeye

   16. Wood light to dark brown to greenish or brownish gray, occasionally pigmented. Rays fine but not constant in size. Wood moderately hard 17

17. Heartwood light to dark brown; sapwood very light tan. Pores close and evenly distributed, appearing solitary in many instances . . . . *Liquidambar styraciflua*
                                                    Red gum

17. Heartwood greenish or brownish gray; sapwood creamy white. Pores in multiples, with a tendency to form irregular radial lines . . . . *Nyssa* spp.
                                                    Black gum; Tupelo gum

   18. Rays extremely fine and constant in size (uniseriate). Pores somewhat larger in earlywood zone. Marginal parenchyma usually evident at margin of growth ring . . 19

   18. Rays easily visible with hand lens and varying in width (multiseriate) 20

19. Wood reddish brown (rays heterocellular) . . . . . . *Salix* spp.
Willow*

19. Wood creamy white to grayish brown
(rays homocellular) . . . . *Populus* spp.
Cottonwood and Aspen†

    20. Rays appearing widely spaced, forming a high and dis-
tinct ray fleck on the radial surface. Wood soft and
light; light tan in color. Occasionally with
distinctive odor . . . . *Tilia* spp.
Basswood

    20. Rays appearing normally spaced, forming a low ray
fleck on radial surface. Wood moderately
hard to hard 21

21. Pores mostly solitary, widest pores
about as wide as widest rays . . . . *Oxydendron arboreum*
Sourwood

21. Pores in multiples and appearing as whitish dots
to the eye. Widest pores wider than
the widest rays . . . . *Betula* spp.
Birch‡

Salix and *Populus* require microscopic study to separate with certainty.

†The cottonwoods and aspens are separated on the basis of texture and color, features which may be quite variable. Cottonwood in medium textured, grayish brown, and non-lustrous. Aspen is fine textured, creamy white, and lustrous.

‡The various birches cannot be separated. Paper birch usually is softer and lighter than others.

APPENDICES

A. SPECIMEN PREPARATION FOR OBSERVATIONS WITH HAND LENS, LIGHT MICROSCOPE, SCANNING ELECTRON MICRO-SCOPE, AND TRANSMISSION ELECTRON MICROSCOPE

Whatever the method of observation used in wood identification, the sample must be prepared appropriately to reveal the evidence needed in the diagnosis. If gross features are being studied, the wood sample should be machined or surfaced so that a fresh sur-face is exposed. Color changes when the wood is exposed to light, to oxidation, or to other agencies. Also, surfacing reveals struc-tural detail that would be masked if the surface were produced by merely splitting the wood. Frequently it is sufficient to simply smooth the surface with a sharp pocket knife so that rays, vessel lines, tissue patterns, and other relatively gross structures can be seen.

Most hand lens observations are made on the transverse sur-face where the cells may be viewed in cross-section. This requires that a clean cut be made with a very sharp blade, preferably a pocket knife which can be controlled with less hazard than a razor blade. However, a single-edge razor blade may be used effectively on some woods. It is occasionally necessary to smooth the tan-gential or radial surfaces of a block of wood for hand lens inspec-tion. An example of this is for finding ripple marks or storied rays in hardwoods.

For light microscopy, thin sections of wood are required. These are prepared with a sliding microtome if permanent micro-scope slides are to be made, but for most routine identification purposes, this time-consuming procedure is not necessary. With practice, one can produce small shavings that are thin enough for light transmission at least on the edges or the tapered end of the shaving. If the surface to be sectioned is first wetted thoroughly, better cuts are possible because of the lubrication provided by the water. Single-edge razor blades can shave thin radial or tangential sections with ease. Cross-sections are rarely possible using this method because the tissue crumbles ahead of the cutting edge.

The wood sections are mounted for temporary use on a clean microscope slide with a drop or two of water, and a cover glass is applied to help flatten the specimen and reduce the drying rate of the water. Actually, at the higher powers of the light microscope it would be difficult to image the structure sharply without a cover glass as the objective lenses are computed for use with this layer of glass over the specimen.

Specimens to be viewed in the scanning electron microscope (SEM) are first surfaced with a microtome or a fresh razor blade and then mounted on a specimen support with a conductive paint or adhesive. They are then coated with evaporated carbon followed by gold-palladium in a high-vacuum evaporator. These thin layers conduct electron charges to ground and minimize "charging" effects. In some models of microscopes, specimens as large as 1 X 1 inch can be accommodated, but porous materials such as wood require very long pumpdown times when the specimens are too large. Much smaller sizes are preferred.

For transmission electron microscopy (TEM) the wood specimens need to be embedded in a hard plastic such as methacrylate or epoxy and then cut to very thin (ultra-thin) sections before the electron beam can be transmitted through the specimen. Generally sections should be about 500 Angstrom units ($\frac{1}{20}$th of a micrometer) thick for acceptable results. With accelerating voltages as high as 100 KV, somewhat thicker sections may be satisfactory.

Surface views of wood may be prepared via transmission electron microscopy by using replication techniques of specimen preparation. These facsimile specimens are composed of nothing more than evaporated metal and carbon, but they provide faithful, high-resolution representations of the wood surfaces.

Both SEM and TEM are better suited to ultrastructural studies than to wood identification, but are useful tools for overall characterization of wood structure as evidenced in many of the illustrations found in this manual.

B. MAGNIFICATION, RESOLUTION, DIMENSIONS;
CELL DIAMETERS AND LENGTHS

MAGNIFICATION

Gross features of wood are important in wood identification, but as pointed out earlier, finer detail is often needed for making the definitive identification. A hand lens magnifies the structure sufficiently to permit positive identification in many cases. This is inadequate for the separation of many of the softwoods, however, and a compound light microscope must be employed to enlarge the structural detail as much as several hundred times to afford clear observation and diagnosis. Seldom would it be necessary to use a scanning electron microscope or a transmission electron microscope for wood identification. These bring the observer into the realm of ultrastructure at the higher magnifications. It is a region of magnification that makes it possible to "see" the components of the cell wall such as cellulose microfibrils.

A hand lens magnifies from 3X to 10X, approximately. The light microscope, with the usual optics, provides a range of 25X to 1000X, on the average. The scanning electron microscope in many cases can magnify detail as little as 7X or as much as 240,000X, although the commonly employed range in wood structure studies might be 15X to 25,000X. The transmission electron microscope generally provides magnification from 1000X to 200,000X, although the make and model of instrument determines whether a broader or narrower range of magnifications is possible.

RESOLUTION

Magnification without resolution is a useless or, at least, limited advantage to the unaided eye. The optical system must have the inherent resolving power for separating detail in the structure as well as magnifying it. In general it is safe to say that the magnification range at which most instruments are employed is determined by the resolving power. The maximum resolving power of the light microscope is 0.2 micrometers. The scanning electron microscope can resolve 100 Angstrom units with ideal specimens. This is equivalent to 1/100th of a micrometer. With the transmission electron microscope it is possible to see structures separated by as little as 10 Angstrom units.

DIMENSIONS

The units of measure employed in microscopy follow the Metric System. Thus a *meter* (39.37 inches) may be divided into 100 *centimeters*. There are 1000 *millimeters* (mm.) in a meter and one million *micrometers* which were formerly called *microns*. Accordingly, each millimeter is composed of 1000 micrometers. There are 10,000 *Angstrom units* in a micrometer.

The concern indicated here for dimensions is based on two factors. First, these units are necessary for calibrating a microscope accurately. The scales or stage micrometers are generally manufactured according to the Metric System.

Secondly, identification is quite often based on the dimensions of structural features such as the diameter of cells. Once the microscope has been calibrated by the method described in Appendix C, it is a simple matter to make such measurements quickly and easily.

CELL DIAMETERS AND LENGTHS

There are published tables available for tracheid lengths of the many coniferous species found in North America. These data provide a handy reference when identifying separate wood cells such as papermaking fibers which have been pulped from wood chips.

Users of this manual who find a need for such tables are referred to publications containing data for the appropriate species. For species native to North America, the *Textbook of Wood Technology*, Volume I, Third Edition, by Panshin and de Zeeuw, is a useful reference.

A few dimensions can be given to indicate the approximate range of cell sizes in the softwoods and hardwoods. As in all natural substances it should be appreciated that considerable variation can be found within a single species, and even within different portions of a single tree.

Average coniferous tracheid length for domestic softwoods ranges from approximately 1.20 mm. to more than 5.4 mm. Tangential diameters of these cells may range from a low of about 15 micrometers to more than 80 micrometers.

Hardwood vessel elements are much shorter cells. Some are no more than .20 mm. long, while the longer ones are somewhat over 1.0 mm. Tangential diameters of vessels, known as pores when viewed on a cross-section, may be less than 50 micrometers up to very large sizes in excess of 300 micrometers, depending upon species.

Other types of hardwood cells will also be found to exhibit wide ranges in size according to the species being examined. Some of these size data may be found in the Panshin and de Zeeuw reference cited above.

C. THE LIGHT MICROSCOPE, ITS CALIBRATION AND USE

INTRODUCTION

The light microscope is an instrument that is readily available in most laboratories and is undoubtedly the instrument of choice for most structural studies. Electron microscopes are both expensive and limiting as to ease of application and specimen preparation. However, as common as the light microscope may be in high school biology classes, university level laboratories, and industrial facilities, it is perhaps the most misused of all familiar instruments.

In the discussion that follows, it must be assumed that the user has taken the time to read the instruction manual that is provided with most microscopes. These manuals usually include a brief review of the theory of the light microscope and suggestions for the effective use of the instrument for normal and for oil immersion applications. Often there is a section on simple methods of specimen preparation. In Appendix A of this manual there is a short description of the simple methods that may be used for preparing wood samples for study.

A few comments on setting up for effective observations with a light microscope would be appropriate. First, the instrument should be placed on a table or desk at a comfortable height so that several hours of use will not create physical strain. The stage and the optics should be free of dust and fingerprints. If the microscope is not equipped with a built-in light source, a microscope illuminator with diffuser to reduce glare would be desirable. However, an ordinary gooseneck lamp with frosted bulb will suffice. The mirror is turned with the flat surface up, not the concave. Light is then directed from the light source to the sub-stage condenser so that the lower condenser lens if filled with light.

The iris diaphragm in the sub-stage condenser may be used for light control in the simplest arrangement, but actually its purpose is to control the cone of light that reaches the objective lens. It should fill the front element of the objective. However, any additional light can be the cause of glare and consequent reduction in apparent image contrast and sharpness.

With a built-in light source, the diaphragm on the light source (called a field diaphragm) controls the amount of light that reaches the condenser, while the sub-stage diaphragm controls the size of the cone reaching the objective lens.

Closing the sub-stage diaphragm somewhat can improve depth of field in the image, but excessive reduction in the size of the opening can lead to diffraction fringes and reduced image quality.

Generally the microscopist focuses on the specimen using the lowest power objective lens. The sub-stage condenser is raised or lowered to fill the field with light. Observations can then go on with this lens or with a higher-powered objective. The expensive microscopes are often parfocalized; that is, all of the objective lenses are close to focus when an objective is changed by revolving the nosepiece. In most cases some minor adjustment may be necessary.

OPTICS

Most moderately priced microscopes are equipped with two or three objective lenses. Some may have four or five, especially as prices or quality categories go up. Usually there is a low-power objective which may be labeled as a 32 mm. or 1X lens. The medium-power objective is marked as 10X or 16mm. In some instances there may be an 8 mm. or 20X objective lens, but this category is less frequently found today. Finally, there is a 4 mm. or 43X objective for high power. All of these lenses are of the so-called "high and dry" variety because they need not be used with oil immersion.

Objectives of 63X and 100X are found on more expensive microscopes, but for the observations described in this manual, they are not essential.

The condenser system on the microscope is designed to provide adequate light control to fill even the high-power objective. It should be provided with a knob that permits raising or lowering of the condenser and iris diaphragm assembly.

The eyepiece, or eyepieces if a binocular microscope is

used, will be of the 10X Huygenian type in most instances. Thus, with 1X, 10X, and 43X objective lenses, the magnification product of most simple microscopes and a 10X eyepiece would be 10X, 100X, and 430X. These values are approximate due to manufacturing variations, and therefore calibration of the individual microscope is advised if measurements are to be made with the instrument.

CALIBRATION PROCEDURE

In wood identification it is often useful to measure certain anatomical features such as cell diameter to eliminate species on a size basis or to confirm a diagnosis with known size data. Only two items are needed besides the microscope itself to calibrate the objective and eyepiece combinations for magnification. First, the eyepiece or ocular must be fitted with an eyepiece micrometer or scale. If you have a binocular microscope, only one of the eyepieces need be so equipped. The eyepiece scale may be left in position for normal microscopy as well as for measurements since it does not distract seriously for visual observations.

Second, a stage micrometer must be available as the "known" or standard scale of dimensions. This is in the form of a microscope slide on which is engraved or etched a scale that is usually 2 mm. in length and divided into 1/100 mm. segments. Thus the space between lines is 10 micrometers. In some models one millimeter may be divided in this way, while the second is divided into 1/10 mm. units.

Calibration consists simply of determining the value or indicated dimension between graduations of the eyepiece micrometer *for each* objective lens on the microscope. In other words, a 32 mm. objective in combination with a 10X eyepiece might yield 40 micrometers per division of the eyepiece scale, while a 16 mm. objective lens with the same eyepiece would produce a greater magnification that is indicated as 15 micrometers per division.

To begin the calibration, select the medium-power objective (16 mm., 10X) and focus on the stage micrometer scale. The eyepiece scale should appear superimposed over the stage micrometer scale. Rotate the eyepiece until this condition is created. Of course the stage micrometer scale should have been centered in the field of view as well.

Now, arbitrarily select a line near each end of the eyepiece scale that coincides with lines on the stage micrometer. Count the number of divisions on the eyepiece scale between lines. Count the number of divisions on the stage micrometer between the lines and convert to micrometers. Remember that the smallest division is equal to 10 micrometers. Find the value of one division on the eyepiece scale and divide into the value in micrometers between the lines on the stage micrometer. For example, the eyepiece scale equals 20 divisions. The stage micrometer has 30 divisions between lines that are coincident with the selected eyepiece scale lines. This is equivalent to 300 micrometers. Divide 300 by 20 to obtain 15 micrometers.

This value, 15 micrometers, is the dimension of any structure that is equivalent to the space between two graduations on the eyepiece scale when the 16 mm. objective lens is used. If two graduations extend across a structure, it has a width or length of 30 micrometers.

Now complete the calibration for each of the other objectives and prepare a chart for quick reference. For comparison purposes, with a 10X eyepiece your values should approximate the following:

1X or 32 mm. objective = 40 micrometers per division
10X or 16 mm. objective = 15 micrometers per division
20X or 8 mm. objective = 7.5 micrometers per division
43X or 4 mm. objective = 3.7 micrometers per division

Occasionally there may be a microscope with a 4X objective. It should calibrate at about 37 micrometers per division of the eyepiece scale. In these determinations just remember that there are 1000 micrometers (microns) per millimeter or 1,000,000 micrometers per meter. Finally, refer to Figure 58 for a graphic example of the use of these two scales.

D. SELF-STUDY DATA FOR INDIVIDUAL SPECIES; GUIDES FOR QUICK REFERENCE

The following descriptive material for individual species or kinds of wood is offered as supplementary material for self-study. The woods selected for this section are primarily available commercially. Some of them, of course, could not be found except in limited areas, close to the sources of supply. For species that are not listed, but may be purchased in a lumber yard occasionally, a

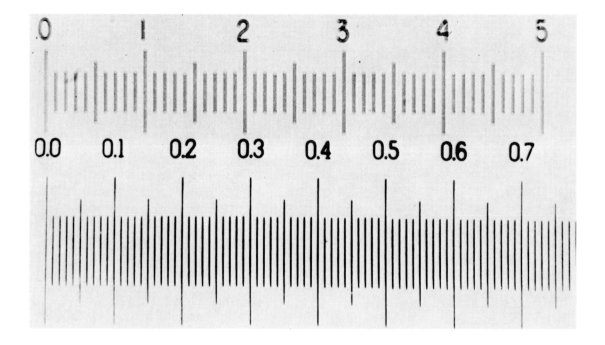

Figure 58. The appearance of the two scales used in calibrating a light microscope. The upper scale is installed in the eyepiece while the lower one is on a stage micrometer. Their images can be positioned as in this photomicrograph and appropriate measurements can then be made.

description may be obtained from one of the many references included in this manual. Examples would be true mahogany (*Swietenia* sp.) or Obeche (*Triplochiton scleroxylon*) which are among many tropical woods being imported into this country.

Most of the features described in these guides are either gross characters that can be observed with the unaided eye or structures that require a hand lens for clearer observation. In either case the surface of the sample should be prepared as indicated in Appendix A. Otherwise, the important characteristics may be masked by surface coatings, oxidation, weathering, or machining marks.

Some microscopic features are included, particularly where it is impossible to identify a wood that closely resembles another. As noted, in some instances, even the use of a light microscope will be of no value in separating two woods of the same genus. In such cases, a generic name can be applied; for example, the "birches".

The individual descriptions are designed to be entered on 3″ X 5″ cards or reproduced on sheets which in turn might be mounted on 3″ X 5″ study blocks of wood. It is hoped that the written description together with the wood sample will increase the benefits of self-study by relating the two more intimately.

Red maple (soft maple)   *Acer rubrum*   ACERACEAE

Color: Heartwood light brown sometimes with a grayish or purplish cast; sapwood wide and white. Wood non-lustrous.
Growth ring pattern: Diffuse-porous; rings delineated by a narrow darker line.
Latewood pore arrangement: Pores small, evenly distributed, solitary and in radial multiples.
Longitudinal parenchyma: Not distinguishable. Marginal, intermingled with fibers.
Rays: Visible to eye, varying uniformly in width; the largest about as wide as the largest pores. Ray fleck conspicuous. Rays appearing as short, crowded lines on tangential surface.
Miscellaneous: Separated from hard maple by appearance of rays and lack of luster.

Sugar maple (hard maple)   *Acer saccharum*   ACERACEAE

Color: Heartwood uniformly reddish brown; sapwood wide and white.
Growth ring pattern: Diffuse-porous; rings delineated by a narrow, darker line.
Latewood pore arrangement: Pores small, evenly distributed; solitary and in radial multiples.
Longitudinal parenchyma: Not visible to eye. Marginal, intermingled with fibers.
Rays: Appearing to be of two widths, the largest as wide or wider than the largest pores and visible to eye. Narrow rays difficult to see with hand lens.
Miscellaneous: Sugar maple is distinguished from soft maple by having rays of two sizes and being lustrous.

American holly   *Ilex opaca*   AQUIFOLIACEAE

Color: Both sapwood and heartwood ivory white; sometimes with a bluish tinge.
Growth ring pattern: Diffuse-porous, the margin of the growth ring made up of denser, fibrous tissue.
Latewood pore arrangement: Pores quite small, arranged in radial chains of multiple pores.
Longitudinal parenchyma: Not visible with hand lens.
Rays: Of two widths; broad rays visible to the eye but not distinct; consistent in distribution. Narrow rays barely visible with hand lens.
Miscellaneous: One of the whitest of commercial woods. A specialty wood.

Red alder   *Alnus rubra*   BETULACEAE

Color: Heartwood aging to flesh tinge or light brown. Sapwood and heartwood not distinct.
Growth ring pattern: Diffuse-porous, rings delineated by whitish or brownish line.
Latewood pore arrangement: Pores numerous, small, in multiples and small clusters.
Longitudinal parenchyma: Not visible except for marginal mixed in with fibers.
Rays: Uniseriate and aggregate; the aggregates of irregular occurrence.
Miscellaneous: Often confused with birch but softer and containing aggregate rays.

Yellow birch   *Betula alleghaniensis*   BETULACEAE

Color: Heartwood light to dark brown; usually reddish brown. Sapwood whitish to
  pale yellow.
Growth ring pattern: Diffuse-porous.
Pore arrangement: Uniformly distributed in multiples of 2–several.
Longitudinal parenchyma: Not visible.
Rays: Evenly distributed, barely visible. Largest rays narrower than widest pores.
Miscellaneous: Pores on cross section frequently appear as whitish flecks. The
  various birches cannot be separated. Yellow birch and sweet birch generally
  are harder and heavier than the others.

River birch   *Betula nigra*   BETULACEAE

Color: Heartwood light to dark brown, usually reddish brown. Sapwood whitish to
  pale yellow.
Growth ring pattern: Diffuse-porous.
Pore arrangement: Uniformly distributed in multiples of 2–several.
Longitudinal parenchyma: Not visible.
Rays: Evenly spaced, barely visible. Largest rays narrower than widest pores.
Miscellaneous: Pores on cross section frequently show as whitish flecks. The vari-
  ous birches cannot be separated with certainty.

American hornbeam   *Carpinus caroliniana*   BETULACEAE

Color: Heartwood pale yellow or brownish. Sapwood thick, whitish.
Growth ring pattern: Diffuse-porous; ring boundary with a narrow, whitish band
  that is somewhat wavy.
Latewood pore arrangement: Pores small, usually in multiples and aggregated into
  clusters that are radially oblique groupings (dendritic).
Longitudinal parenchyma: Apotracheal and marginal; the apotracheal somewhat
  indistinct with a lens.
Rays: Both large (aggregate) and narrow (simple) present. Large rays indistinct due
  to being nearly the color of the background.
Miscellaneous: Hard and heavy; sometimes confused with holly.

Hophornbeam   *Ostrya virginiana*   BETULACEAE

Color: Heartwood usually light brown, sometimes tinged with red.
Growth ring pattern: Diffuse-porous; ring margins with scattered specks of paren-
  chyma. Ring margins inconspicuous.
Latewood pore arrangement: Pores small, solitary and in multiples; usually aggre-
  gated into radially oblique groups or patches (dendritic).
Longitudinal parenchyma: Apotracheal, visible with lens; more abundant in outer
  portion of ring.
Rays: Fine and indistinct. Crowded; appearing to occupy half of surface area.
Miscellaneous: Hard and heavy.

Catalpa   *Catalpa speciosa; C. bignonioides*   BIGNONIACEAE

Color: Heartwood grayish brown to brown; sapwood narrow.
Growth ring pattern: Semi-ring-porous to ring-porous, the earlywood zone wide. Individual rings frequently variable in width.
Latewood pore arrangement: Latewood pores small, in small groups; coalescing in short to long bands in outer margin.
Longitudinal parenchyma: When distinct, associated with pores in outer margin of ring (paratracheal).
Rays: Indistinct to eye. Normally spaced.
Miscellaneous: Heartwood with distinctive odor, slightly aromatic or musty.

Dogwood   *Cornus florida*   CORNACEAE

Color: Sapwood (commercial lumber) carneous to light pinkish brown (flesh colored); heartwood narrow, dark brown.
Growth ring pattern: Diffuse-porous; growth rings not sharply defined.
Latewood pore arrangement: Pores small, frequently solitary or in radial multiples.
Longitudinal parenchyma: Apotracheal, indistinct and mostly in outer portion of ring.
Rays: Of two widths; not conspicuous due to color of background.
Miscellaneous: Difficult to separate from hard maple; the flesh color of sapwood and the apotracheal parenchyma are useful features.

Tupelo gum   *Nyssa aquatica*   CORNACEAE

Color: White to grayish sapwood; heartwood greenish to brownish gray.
Growth ring pattern: Diffuse-porous; rings indistinct.
Latewood pore arrangement: Pores small, uniform in size, numerous with a tendency to form short radial groups and multiples. Somewhat irregular in distribution.
Longitudinal parenchyma: None visible.
Rays: Fine and close; appearing to occupy half of surface.
Miscellaneous: Grain usually interlocked. The tendency to form pore multiples and the larger size of the rays help to distinguish from redgum.
Swamp tupelo, *Nyssa sylvatica* var. *biflora,* is similar.

Blackgum   *Nyssa sylvatica*   CORNACEAE

Color: White to grayish sapwood; sapwood very wide. Heartwood greenish to brownish gray.
Growth ring pattern: Diffuse-porous; rings indistinct.
Latewood pore arrangement: Pores small, uniform in size, numerous with a tendency to form radial groups and multiples.
Longitudinal parenchyma: None visible.
Rays: Fine and close; appearing to occupy one-half of surface.
Miscellaneous: Grain interlocked. Usually firmer and denser than tupelo gum. Wood is prone to blue stain.

Persimmon   *Diospyros virginiana*   EBENACEAE

Color: Sapwood very wide; creamy or yellowish white when cut, turning darker
    sometimes staining gray. Heartwood very small, black or blackish brown.
Growth ring pattern: Semi-ring-porous, earlywood pores barely visible to eye.
Latewood pore arrangement: Pores scattered, solitary or in multiples, thick-walled.
Longitudinal parenchyma: Apotracheal-banded, conspicuous with a lens, appearing
    as closely spaced lines (netlike) between the rays.
Rays: Not visible or barely visible to eye. Rays storied, forming ripple marks on the
    tangential surface.
Miscellaneous: The classic wood for turning, where toughness, hardness and im-
    pact resistance are desired.

Pacific madrone   *Arbutus menziesii*   ERICACEAE

Color: Heartwood light reddish brown. Sapwood whitish or with pinkish cast.
Growth ring pattern: Diffuse or semi-ring-porous; the first-formed row of early-
    wood pores larger and in a somewhat continuous row.
Latewood pore arrangement: Pores quite numerous and small; solitary or in multi-
    ples and radial rows with a tendency to band tangentially.
Longitudinal parenchyma: Not visible.
Rays: Visible with lens; normally spaced.
Miscellaneous: Hard and heavy. Of limited use at present.

American chestnut   *Castanea dentata*   FAGACEAE

Color: Heartwood grayish brown to brown.
Growth ring pattern: Ring-porous. Earlywood pores large and conspicuous. Tyloses
    numerous.
Latewood pore arrangement: Dendritic, pores in patches of light colored tissue.
Longitudinal parenchyma: Indistinct; paratracheal and apotracheal.
Rays: Fine, not visible to unaided eye; normally spaced.
Miscellaneous: Resembles oaks except for absence of large rays.

Beech   *Fagus grandifolia*   FAGACEAE

Color: Heartwood with a reddish tinge; sapwood whitish.
Growth ring pattern: Diffuse-porous. A denser, narrow band of latewood is fre-
    quently visible at the margin of the growth ring. Tyloses present.
Latewood pore arrangement: Pores small, numerous, solitary and in radial multi-
    ples. Decreasing in size and numbers through the latewood.
Longitudinal parenchyma: Not distinguishable with a hand lens or appearing as
    finely punctate lines in the latewood.
Rays: Of two sizes; broad oak-type plainly visible to the eye, separated by fine rays
    that are not visible without magnification.
Miscellaneous: Broad rays appear on the tangential surface as relatively widely
    spaced, staggered lines that are visible to the eye.

Tanoak   *Lithocarpus densiflorus*   FAGACEAE

Color: Sapwood wide, light reddish brown. Heartwood light brown to dark reddish
brown.
Growth ring pattern: Semi-ring-porous, transition in pore size quite gradual.
Latewood pore arrangement: Pores in somewhat oblique groups or clusters; un-
evenly distributed.
Longitudinal parenchyma: Apotracheal banded, abundant and visible with hand
lens as irregular wide lines.
Rays: Of two sizes; the broad rays irregular in distribution.
Miscellaneous: Limited in commercial use at present.

Red oak   *Quercus rubra* and other species   FAGACEAE

Color: Heartwood light, reddish brown or pinkish brown, usually with a flesh-
colored tinge.
Growth ring pattern: Ring-porous; transition more or less abrupt. Earlywood pores
large; in 1–4 rows. Tyloses rare.
Latewood pore arrangement: Dendritic; concentrated in groups associated with
light-colored tissue. Rounded and thick-walled.
Longitudinal parenchyma: Abundant; both paratracheal and apotracheal.
Rays: Of two sizes; broad and conspicuous and narrow and inconspicuous.
Miscellaneous: Cannot be separated with certainty from other red oaks.

White oak   *Quercus alba* and other species   FAGACEAE

Color: Light brown to dark brown.
Growth ring pattern: Ring-porous; transition more or less abrupt. Earlywood pores
large, in 1–3 rows. Tyloses usually abundant.
Latewood pore arrangement: Concentrated in irregular patches of light-colored
tissue. Dendritic. Pores small, numerous, and with angular margins.
Longitudinal parenchyma: Paratracheal and apotracheal, paratracheal forming
patches of tissue in which the latewood pores are located.
Rays: Of two types: broad and conspicuous and narrow and inconspicuous.
Miscellaneous: Distinguished from red oaks by: (1) latewood pores small, angular
and thin-walled; (2) abundant tyloses; (3) higher rays.

Redgum   *Liquidambar styraciflua*   HAMAMELIDACEAE

Color: Sapwood (called sapgum) whitish with a pinkish tinge, often with blue stain
attack. Heartwood with considerable variation; carneous gray to dark red-
dish brown. Often with darker streaks of pigment.
Growth ring pattern: Diffuse-porous; growth rings indistinct.
Latewood pore arrangement: Pores small, uniform in size and distribution; essen-
tially solitary.
Longitudinal parenchyma: None visible.
Rays: Fine and very close; appearing to occupy half the surface area.
Miscellaneous: Rarely with longitudinal gum canals (wound). Extensively used in
wood market.

Yellow buckeye   *Aesculus octandra*   HIPPOCASTANACEAE

Color: Heartwood creamy white to pale yellowish white, often with grayish streaks; very susceptible to blue stain.
Growth ring pattern: Diffuse-porous, marginal parenchyma showing as a fine, light-colored line.
Latewood pore arrangement: Pores numerous, extremely small. Not visible to eye. Solitary and in multiples.
Longitudinal parenchyma: Marginal.
Rays: Extremely narrow (uniseriate), usually storied forming ripple marks on the tangential surface.
Miscellaneous: Ohio buckeye normally will not show ripple marks. Wood very light and soft.

True hickory   *Carya ovata* & other species   JUGLANDACEAE

Color: Heartwood pale brown to brown or reddish brown.
Growth ring pattern: Ring-porous. Abrupt transition.
Latewood pore arrangement: Irregularly spaced, solitary and in radial multiples of 2–3.
Longitudinal parenchyma: Apotracheal banded and marginal. Conspicuous as parallel white lines forming a ladder arrangement with the rays in the latewood.
Rays: Normally spaced, not visible without lens.
Miscellaneous: Hard, heavy. Tyloses common in earlywood.

Pecan hickory   *Carya illinoensis*   JUGLANDACEAE

Color: Heartwood pale brown to brown or reddish brown, occasionally with darker zones.
Growth ring pattern: Semi-ring-porous.
Latewood pore arrangement: Irregularly spaced, solitary, or in radial multiples of 2–several.
Longitudinal parenchyma: Apotracheal banded and marginal. Apotracheal parenchyma conspicuous as parallel white lines forming a ladder-like arrangement with rays in the latewood, usually extending into earlywood zone.
Rays: Barely visible to unaided eye, normally spaced.
Miscellaneous: Hard, heavy. Tyloses visible in earlywood.

Butternut   *Juglans cinerea*   JUGLANDACEAE

Color: Heartwood light chestnut brown, usually with flesh colored tinge. Sapwood light grayish brown.
Growth ring pattern: Semi-ring-porous. Latewood and earlywood pores of adjacent rings with abrupt change in size. Tyloses common.
Latewood pore arrangement: Pores scattered; solitary and in radial multiples.
Longitudinal parenchyma: Apotracheal; more apparent in outer portion of ring; in fine, continuous lines.
Rays: Fine, normally spaced. Indistinct to eye.
Miscellaneous: Soft and light. Easily cut and dented.

Black walnut   *Juglans nigra*   JUGLANDACEAE

Color: Heartwood light brown to rich chocolate; frequently with purplish cast.
Growth ring pattern: Semi-ring-porous. Latewood pores sharply defined from early-
    wood pores of adjacent ring.
Latewood pore arrangement: Solitary and in radial multiples of 2–several. Scattered.
    Tyloses common.
Longitudinal parenchyma: Apotracheal in fine, continuous lines. Indistinct to eye.
Rays: Fine; indistinct to eye.
Miscellaneous: Has slight nut-like odor. Color is distinctive.

Sassafras   *Sassafras albidum*   LAURACEAE

Color: Heartwood dark brown, dull grayish brown or orange brown.
Growth ring pattern: Ring-porous. Transition abrupt. Earlywood pores large, in 3–8
    rows; frequently with glistening tyloses.
Latewood pore arrangement: Pores solitary and in multiples of 2–3, relatively numer-
    ous.
Longitudinal parenchyma: Paratracheal and aliform; forming a thick, indistinct ring
    or band.
Rays: Visible to eye; appearing uniform in size and spacing.
Miscellaneous: Spicy, distinctive odor. Separated from the ashes by abundance of
    latewood pores, more pronounced aliform parenchyma and spicy odor.

Oregon-myrtle   *Umbellularia californica*   LAURACEAE
California-laurel

Color: Heartwood light brown to grayish brown, frequently with darker streaks.
Growth ring pattern: Diffuse-porous, rings distinct due to denser fibrous zone.
Pore arrangement: Pores small, indistinct and scattered, evenly distributed; solitary
    and in multiples of 2–several.
Longitudinal parenchyma: Paratracheal, forming a thickened sheath around the
    vessels.
Rays: Not distinct to the eye; uniformly spaced.
Miscellaneous: A characteristic, sometimes strong, spicy odor is present. The wood
    is reported to darken appreciably when soaked in water and then dried.

Redbud   *Cercis canadensis*   LEGUMINOSAE

Color: Heartwood light brown to reddish brown, usually with a golden luster.
Growth ring pattern: Ring-porous; earlywood consisting of several rows.
Latewood pore arrangement: Pores usually in wavy tangential (ulmiform) bands;
    occasionally echelon. No tyloses present.
Longitudinal parenchyma: Marginal and paratracheal confluent; the confluent pa-
    renchyma difficult to distinguish.
Rays: Visible to eye on surface; distinct on radial surface; rays storied forming close
    ripple marks on tangential surface.
Miscellaneous: All elements storied. Wood of local use only.

Yellowwood   *Cladrastis lutea*   LEGUMINOSAE

Color: Fresh heartwood clear yellow; darkening to light brown.
Growth ring pattern: Semi-ring-porous to diffuse-porous. Earlywood pores frequently in a single, more or less continuous row.
Latewood pore arrangement: Pores small, solitary, in multiples and occasionally in nests.
Longitudinal parenchyma: Paratracheal, giving a thick-walled effect to latewood pores. Also marginal and apotracheal.
Rays: Visible to naked eye, moderately spaced.

Honeylocust   *Gleditsia triacanthos*   LEGUMINOSAE

Color: Heartwood reddish brown or light red; reddish cast usually obvious.
Growth-ring pattern: Ring-porous, transition abrupt. Earlywood pores large, in 3–5 rows. Frequently with deposits of reddish gum. Tyloses absent.
Latewood pore arrangement: Pores small, solitary, in radial lines and in nest-like groups.
Longitudinal parenchyma: Paratracheal and paratracheal-confluent, particularly in the last formed latewood.
Rays: Appearing of two different sizes, the larger easily visible to the unaided eye.
Miscellaneous: Distinguished from Kentucky coffeetree by two sizes of rays, paratracheal-confluent parenchyma in edge of latewood and presence of gum deposits in vessels.

Kentucky coffeetree   *Gymnocladus dioicus*   LEGUMINOSAE

Color: Heartwood reddish to reddish brown.
Growth ring pattern: Ring-porous; earlywood pores large, in 3–6 rows. Tyloses absent. Reddish gum rarely present.
Latewood pore arrangement: Pores in nestlike groups and occasionally coalescing in outer margin.
Longitudinal parenchyma: Not visible to eye.
Rays: Visible to eye; normally spaced and uniform in size.
Miscellaneous: Frequently confused with honeylocust.

Black locust   *Robinia pseudoacacia*   LEGUMINOSAE

Color: Heartwood greenish yellow to golden brown.
Growth ring pattern: Ring-porous with 2–3 rows of earlywood pores. Earlywood pores completely occluded with tyloses.
Latewood pore arrangement: In nestlike groups that frequently coalesce in outer portion.
Longitudinal parenchyma: Not distinct to eye.
Rays: Small, normally spaced. Usually visible to eye.
Miscellaneous: Very hard and heavy. Confused with mulberry and Osage orange.

Yellowpoplar   *Liriodendron tulipifera*   MAGNOLIACEAE

Color: Variable; shades of brown and greenish brown, occasionally purplish
brown. Sapwood whitish, often called whitewood.
Growth ring pattern: Diffuse-porous.
Pore arrangement: Pores uniformly spaced; numerous in radial multiples of 2–sev-
eral.
Longitudinal parenchyma: Marginal; visible as a conspicuous white line.
Rays: Visible to unaided eye on cross section, uniform in size and spacing, relatively
closely spaced. Ray fleck low and close on radial surface.
Miscellaneous: Relatively light and soft. Similar in appearance to *Magnolia* spp.

Cucumber   *Magnolia acuminata*   MAGNOLIACEAE

Color: Sapwood white; heartwood variable, ranging from light yellow, greenish
yellow, brown to greenish black,
Growth ring pattern: Diffuse-porous; margin of ring delineated by a conspicuous
whitish line of parenchyma.
Latewood pore arrangement: Pores small, uniform in size and distribution; usually
in multiples of 2–several.
Longitudinal parenchyma: Marginal, appearing as a whitish line.
Rays: Distinct to the naked eye, appearing uniform in width and normally distributed.
Miscellaneous: Difficult if not impossible to separate from magnolia and
yellowpoplar.

Magnolia   *Magnolia grandiflora*   MAGNOLIACEAE

Color: Sapwood white; heartwood yellow, greenish yellow, brown to greenish
black.
Growth ring pattern: Diffuse-porous; margin of ring distinct due to a conspicuous
whitish line of parenchyma.
Latewood pore arrangement: Pores small, uniform in size and distribution; in multi-
ples of 2–several.
Longitudinal parenchyma: Marginal, appearing as a whitish line.
Rays: Distinct; uniform and normally distributed.
Miscellaneous: Harder and heavier than yellowpoplar and cucumber but difficult
to separate. Marginal parenchyma lines and rays usually wider in this wood.
May be separated with microscopic features.

Osage orange   *Maclura pomifera*   MORACEAE

Color: Heartwood golden-yellow to orange to dark golden-brown. Coloring matter
soluble in warm water giving a yellowish hue.
Growth ring pattern: Ring-porous; transition abrupt. Earlywood pores in 2–3 rows.
Pores completely occluded with tyloses. Pore outlines indistinct.
Latewood pore arrangement: In nestlike groups, sometimes confluent in outer mar-
gins.
Longitudinal parenchyma: Paratracheal and paratracheal confluent.
Rays: Visible to eye.
Miscellaneous: Difficult to separate from black locust. Best features are coloring
matter and indistinct pore margins.

Red mulberry   *Morus rubra*   MORACEAE

Color: Heartwood orange-yellow when freshly cut, aging to golden-brown or rus-set-brown.
Growth ring pattern: Ring-porous, the earlywood pores in several rows. Earlywood pores large and plainly visible to eye.
Latewood pore arrangement: Pores in nestlike groups, the groups close and appearing more or less as wavy, concentric bands (ulmiform).
Longitudinal parenchyma: Not visible.
Rays: Plainly visible to eye, normally spaced; forming a conspicuous fleck on the radial surface.
Miscellaneous: Abundant tyloses and lustrous brown color usually help to identify this wood.

White ash   *Fraxinus americana*   OLEACEAE

Color: Heartwood grayish brown; light brown streaked with darker brown or light yellow.
Growth ring pattern: Ring-porous; transition abrupt. Earlywood pores in 2–4 rows. Tyloses common.
Latewood pore arrangement: Pores small, solitary and in multiples of 2–3.
Longitudinal parenchyma: Paratracheal, encircling latewood pores, and coalescing in outer margin.
Rays: Not visible to eye.
Miscellaneous: Wood firm, lustrous, straight grained.

Black ash, brown ash   *Fraxinus nigra*   OLEACEAE

Color: Sapwood narrow. Heartwood grayish brown or brown and non-lustrous.
Growth ring pattern: Ring-porous, earlywood pores quite large and visible to eye, 2–4 pores wide.
Latewood pore arrangement: Latewood zone usually narrow due to growth conditions. Pores widely scattered, solitary and radial multiples of 2–4.
Longitudinal parenchyma: Paratracheal, encircling latewood pores as a sheath, rarely joining pores in outer margin of ring.
Rays: Not visible to eye, normally spaced.
Miscellaneous: May be confused with white ash. Typical examples are lighter, weaker and less lustrous than white ash as well as having very narrow growth rings.

Sycamore   *Platanus occidentalis*   PLATANACEAE

Color: Sapwood white to yellowish; heartwood brown to reddish brown.
Growth ring pattern: Diffuse-porous; margin delineated by a band of lighter tissue.
Latewood pore arrangement: Pores small and indistinct, numerous and often crowded with a tendency to tangential pairing.
Longitudinal parenchyma: None visible.
Rays: Fairly wide and conspicuous; appearing uniform in width and distribution. The rays form a conspicuous fleck on the radial surface and appear as closely packed lines on the tangential surface.
Miscellaneous: Sometimes confused with beech.

Buckthorn   *Rhamnus caroliniana*   RHAMNACEAE

Color: Sapwood yellowish and wide. Heartwood yellowish brown frequently tinged with red.
Growth ring pattern: Semi-ring-porous; earlywood pores small, frequently in a single uniseriate row.
Latewood pore arrangement: Pores small, solitary, and in multiples, somewhat scattered.
Longitudinal parenchyma: Not visible to eye or appearing as partial, whitish flecks around pores.
Rays: Visible to eye; uniform in size and normally spaced.
Miscellaneous: Cascara buckthorn, *R. purshiana*, from West Coast is similar. Neither are commercial woods.

Black cherry   *Prunus serotina*   ROSACEAE

Color: Heartwood light reddish brown, occasionally dark red brown. Non-lustrous.
Growth ring pattern: Somewhat semi-ring-porous; the first row of earlywood pores somewhat larger in a more or less continuous row. Tyloses absent; gum present in some pores.
Latewood pore arrangement: Solitary, in multiples and in nests forming a somewhat oblique pattern.
Longitudinal parenchyma: Not visible to eye.
Rays: Plainly visible to eye; appearing uniform in size.
Miscellaneous: Longitudinal, traumatic gum canals may be present appearing as dark lines on longitudinal surfaces.

Eastern cottonwood   *Populus deltoides*   SALICACEAE

Color: Heartwood not clearly defined; grayish white to light grayish brown.
Growth ring pattern: Semi-ring (semi-diffuse)-porous. Occasionally approaching diffuse-porous.
Latewood pore arrangement: Pores small, uniformly and closely spaced; in radial multiples of 2–several.
Longitudinal parenchyma: Marginal, visible as a narrow, light-colored line.
Rays: Fine, not visible to unaided eye. Normally spaced.
Miscellaneous: Relatively light and soft. Occasionally foul-smelling when wet.
The various aspens and cottonwoods sometimes are separated on the basis of texture, but this is difficult.

Black willow   *Salix nigra*   SALICACEAE

Color: Reddish brown, grayish brown, or light brown, nearly always with brownish cast in heartwood. Often streaked.
Growth ring pattern: Semi-ring (semi-diffuse)-porous.
Latewood pore arrangement: Pores small, numerous, closely spaced, solitary and in multiples of 2–several.
Longitudinal parenchyma: Marginal, not very conspicuous.
Rays: Narrow, not visible to unaided eye. Normally spaced.
Miscellaneous: Light and soft.

Basswood   *Tilia americana*   TILIACEAE
                          Tilia heterophylla

Color: Creamy white to pale brown.
Growth ring pattern: Diffuse-porous; rings distinct due to marginal parenchyma.
Latewood pore arrangement: Pores small, evenly distributed, forming tangential
        and radial groupings which give a lace-like pattern to surface.
Longitudinal parenchyma: Marginal; appearing as a white line; apotracheal in short
        lines which are not visible with lens.
Rays: Appearing widely spaced and forming a high, distant or scattered ray fleck on
        the radial surface.
Miscellaneous: Soft and light. A characteristic odor is recognized by some persons.

Hackberry   *Celtis occidentalis*   ULMACEAE

Color: Heartwood yellowish gray or brown; frequently with a greenish cast. Sap-
        wood pale yellow or greenish yellow.
Growth ring pattern: Ring-porous. Earlywood pores in 2–5 rows.
Latewood pore arrangement: Ulmiform, more or less continuous.
Longitudinal parenchyma: Not visible to eye.
Rays: Distinct to eye.
Miscellaneous: Distinguished from elms by distinctiveness of rays and by color. The
        Celtis species are indistinguishable.

American elm   *Ulmus americana*   ULMACEAE

Color: Heartwood light brown to brown, sometimes reddish.
Growth ring pattern: Ring-porous; transition abrupt. Earlywood pores usually in a
        single, continuous row, visible to eye.
Latewood pore arrangement: Ulmiform, distinct, and continuous.
Longitudinal parenchyma: Not visible to eye.
Rays: Not distinct to eye.
Miscellaneous: Wood usually has interlocked grain.

Slippery elm (red elm)   *Ulmus rubra*   ULMACEAE

Color: Heartwood brown to dark brown or reddish brown. Sapwood grayish white
        to light brown.
Growth ring pattern: Ring-porous. Transition abrupt. Earlywood pores large in 2–4
        rows. Tyloses present.
Latewood pore arrangement: Ulmiform but somewhat indistinct to eye due to color
        of background.
Longitudinal parenchyma: Not visible to eye.
Rays: Indistinct to just visible to eye.
Miscellaneous: Wetted heartwood frequently has disagreeable odor.

Hard elm   *Ulmus thomasii*   ULMACEAE

Color: Sapwood narrow, light brown; heartwood light brown to brown or with
reddish tinge.
Growth ring pattern: Ring-porous. Earlywood pores restricted to a single, inter-
rupted row, the larger pores separated by smaller pores.
Latewood pore arrangement: Pores in wavy, concentric (ulmiform) bands.
Longitudinal parenchyma: Not visible.
Rays: Not distinct to eye.
Miscellaneous: Wood hard and heavy. Grain interlocked.

Northern white pine   *Pinus strobus*   PINACEAE

Color: Heartwood light brown to reddish brown aging to dark reddish brown on
exposure.
Growth ring pattern: Transition gradual. Latewood zone narrow and darker than
earlywood. Wood medium textured.
Longitudinal parenchyma: Not visible. Absent or extremely rare.
Rays: Of two widths, fusiform and uniseriate. The two widths visible with lens on
moist surface.
Miscellaneous: Contains resin canals. Resin canals large and visible to eye. Numerous and present in every growth ring. Wood with faint resinous odor.

Western white pine   *Pinus monticola*   PINACEAE

Color: Heartwood tan to light brown to reddish brown.
Growth ring pattern: Transition gradual. Latewood zone narrow and darker than
earlywood. Wood medium to coarse textured.
Longitudinal parenchyma: Not visible. Absent or extremely rare.
Rays: Of two widths, fusiform and uniseriate. The two widths visible with lens on
moist surface.
Miscellaneous: Contains resin canals. Resin canals usually visible to eye. Numerous
and present in every growth ring. Wood with faint resinous odor.

Sugar pine   *Pinus lambertiana*   PINACEAE

Color: Heartwood light brown to pale reddish brown.
Growth ring pattern: Transition gradual. Latewood zone narrow and darker than
earlywood. Wood coarse textured.
Longitudinal parenchyma: Not visible. Absent or extremely rare.
Rays: Of two widths, fusiform and uniseriate. The two widths visible with lens on
moist surface. Wide rays relatively common.
Miscellaneous: Contains resin canals. Resin canals large and visible to eye. Numer-
ous and present in every growth ring. Wood with faint resinous odor.

Lodgepole pine   *Pinus contorta*   PINACEAE

Color: Heartwood yellow to yellowish brown.
Growth ring pattern: Transition semi-abrupt to abrupt, the latewood usually narrow, not appreciably harder than earlywood to cutting.
Longitudinal parenchyma: Not visible. Absent or extremely rare.
Rays: Of two widths, fusiform and uniseriate. The two widths visible with lens on moist surface. Wide rays sporadic and widely spaced.
Miscellaneous: Contains resin canals. Wood usually contains dimple marks caused by indentations in the growth increments. These may be seen on split tangential surface. Wood with distinct resinous odor.

Red pine   *Pinus resinosa*   PINACEAE

Color: Heartwood light red to orange red.
Growth ring pattern: Semi-abrupt. Latewood zone narrow to wide.
Longitudinal parenchyma: Not visible. Absent or extremely rare.
Rays: Of two widths, fusiform and uniseriate. The wide rays visible with lens on moist surface.
Miscellaneous: Contains resin canals. Resin canals small and numerous in outer portion of ring. Wood with distinct resinous odor.

Ponderosa pine   *Pinus ponderosa*   PINACEAE

Color: Yellowish to light reddish brown.
Growth ring pattern: Transition abrupt. Latewood band width variable, ranging from narrow to wide, sometimes resembling soft pine.
Longitudinal parenchyma: Not visible. Absent or extremely rare.
Rays: Of two widths, fusiform and uniseriate. The two widths visible with lens on moist surface. Wide rays common.
Miscellaneous: Contains resin canals. Resin canals relatively large and visible to eye. Relatively numerous and present in every growth ring. Wood with distinct resinous odor.

Southern yellow pine   *Pinus* sp.   PINACEAE

Color: Heartwood variable in color ranging in shades of yellow through reddish brown.
Growth ring pattern: Transition abrupt. Latewood band variable, frequently wide forming a dense, dark-colored band.
Longitudinal parenchyma: Not visible. Absent or extremely rare.
Rays: Of two widths, fusiform and uniseriate. The two widths visible with lens on moist cross section. Wide rays relatively common.
Miscellaneous: Contains resin canals. Resin canals large and visible to eye. Numerous and present in each ring. Wood with strong resinous odor.

Eastern spruce   *Picea* sp.   PINACEAE

Color: Heartwood nearly white to yellowish brown. Wood lustrous.
Growth ring pattern: Transition gradual, the latewood zone usually very narrow and
    darker than the earlywood.
Longitudinal parenchyma: Not visible. Absent or extremely rare.
Rays: Of two widths, fusiform and uniseriate. The two widths visible with hand
    lens on moist surface. Wide rays sporadic and widely spaced.
Miscellaneous: Contains resin canals. Resin canals small varying in occurrence.
    Appearing as small white dots on cross section.

Engelman spruce   *Picea engelmannii*   PINACEAE

Color: Creamy yellow to yellowish brown, lustrous.
Growth ring pattern: Transition semi-gradual to gradual. Latewood zone distinct
    from earlywood.
Longitudinal parenchyma: Not visible. Absent or extremely rare.
Rays: Of two widths, fusiform and uniseriate. The two widths visible with lens on
    moist surface. Wide rays sporadic and widely spaced.
Miscellaneous: Contains resin canals. Resin canals small, varying in occurrence
    appearing as small white dots on cross section. Usually not separated from
    eastern spruce.

Sitka spruce   *Picea sitchensis*   PINACEAE

Color: Heartwood brownish to purplish brown with a somewhat lustrous appear-
    ance.
Growth ring pattern: Transition semi-gradual to gradual, the latewood distinctly
    darker and denser than earlywood.
Longitudinal parenchyma: Not visible. Absent or extremely rare.
Rays: Of two widths, fusiform and uniseriate; the two widths visible with lens on
    moist surface. Wide rays sporadic and widely spaced.
Miscellaneous: Contains resin canals. Resin canals relatively large and often numer-
    ous.

Eastern larch   *Larix laricina*   PINACEAE

Color: Heartwood yellowish to reddish brown.
Growth ring pattern: Transition abrupt, latewood zone conspicuous.
Longitudinal parenchyma: Not visible. Absent or extremely rare.
Rays: Of two widths, fusiform and uniseriate; the two widths visible. The wide rays
    sporadic and widely spaced.
Miscellaneous: Contains resin canals. Resin canals very sporadic.

Western larch   *Larix occidentalis*   PINACEAE

Color: Heartwood reddish brown.
Growth ring pattern: Transition very abrupt. Latewood zone very narrow and conspicuous.
Longitudinal parenchyma: Not visible. Absent or rarely marginal.
Rays: Of two widths, fusiform and uniseriate; the two widths visible with lens on moist surface. Fusiform rays may be visible as reddish dots on the tangential surface. The wide rays widely spaced.
Miscellaneous: Contains resin canals. Resin canals sporadic, frequently in tangential groups.

Douglas-fir   *Pseudotsuga menziesii*   PINACEAE

Color: Variable, yellowish to orange-red or deep red.
Growth ring pattern: Transition abrupt, latewood zone ranging from narrow to wide.
Longitudinal parenchyma: Not visible. Absent or rarely marginal.
Rays: Of two widths, fusiform and uniseriate; the two widths visible with lens on moist surface. The wide rays widely spaced.
Miscellaneous: Contains resin canals. Resin canals sporadic, frequently in tangential groups in latewood. Helical thickening easily seen with microscope. Wood with distinctive odor.

Balsam fir   *Abies balsamea*   PINACEAE

Color: Creamy white to pale brown, the latewood portion of the growth ring often with a lavender cast.
Growth ring pattern: Transition gradual, latewood distinct due to color. Medium textured.
Longitudinal parenchyma: Not visible. Absent or extremely rare.
Rays: Very fine.
Miscellaneous: Occasionally with unusual but not distinctive odor. Light and soft.

Western fir   *Abies* sp.   PINACEAE

Color: Light buff to light brown, the latewood portion of the growth ring somewhat purplish.
Growth ring pattern: Transition gradual.
Longitudinal parenchyma: Not visible. Absent or extremely rare.
Rays: Very fine.
Miscellaneous: Difficult to separate as to species and from western hemlock. Refer to minute anatomy. Ray tracheids normally are absent and the cross field pits are taxodioid.

Eastern hemlock   *Tsuga canadensis*   PINACEAE

Color: Buff to light brown, the latewood portion of the ring purplish.
Growth ring pattern: Transition variable. Semi-abrupt to abrupt. Ring widths variable from narrow to wide. Latewood distinct to the eye.
Longitudinal parenchyma: Not visible. Absent or extremely rare.
Rays: Very fine.
Miscellaneous: Wood is somewhat brash with a harsh, dry feel. Large pieces of lumber frequently contain ring shakes. May be separated from the firs by the presence of ray tracheids.

Western hemlock   *Tsuga heterophylla*   PINACEAE

Color: Yellowish brown, the latewood portion of the ring purplish.
Growth ring pattern: Transition gradual to semi-abrupt.
Longitudinal parenchyma: Not visible. Absent or extremely rare.
Rays: Very fine.
Miscellaneous: Similar to eastern hemlock but less brash and dry in feel and of better quality. May be separated from the firs by the presence of ray tracheids.

Alaska cedar   *Chamaecyparis nootkatensis*   CUPRESSACEAE

Color: Heartwood bright yellow, darkening to a tannish-yellow on exposure. Sapwood yellowish white.
Growth ring pattern: Evenly fine to medium textured. Growth rings inconspicuous. Usually very narrow rings.
Longitudinal parenchyma: Inconspicuous and usually not visible with hand lens.
Rays: Narrow and inconspicuous.
Miscellaneous: Odor resembling that of raw potatoes. Very characteristic. Straight grained wood.

Port Orford cedar   *Chamaecyparis lawsoniana*   CUPRESSACEAE

Color: Heartwood yellowish white to brownish yellow; sapwood nearly white, not clearly distinguishable from the heartwood.
Growth ring pattern: Transition nearly gradual. Growth rings distinct. Wood even textured.
Longitudinal parenchyma: Abundant, frequently visible with hand lens on wetted surface. Appearing as reddish lines or zones.
Rays: Narrow.
Miscellaneous: Wood with characteristic ginger odor, often with spicy or bitter taste. Wood straight grained.

Eastern red cedar   *Juniperus virginiana*   CUPRESSACEAE

Color: Sapwood white, heartwood purplish red, aging to dull red when exposed.
Growth ring pattern: Growth rings usually evident, transition gradual. Wood very fine textured.
Longitudinal parenchyma: Visible as several dark bands or lines, especially in sapwood material.
Rays: Fine, darker than background in heartwood.
Miscellaneous: Odor "cedary" and characteristic. Grain straight. Sapwood and heartwood usually are mixed to give familiar redcedar appearance.

Incense-cedar   *Libocedrus decurrens*   CUPRESSACEAE

Color: Heartwood reddish brown or dull brown.
Growth ring pattern: Growth rings distinct; transition gradual.
Longitudinal parenchyma: Frequently visible in latewood as dark reddish zones or bands.
Rays: Fine, easily visible with hand lens.
Miscellaneous: Odor pungent and spicy. Taste acrid. Straight grained.

Northern white cedar   *Thuja occidentalis*   CUPRESSACEAE

Color: Heartwood straw-brown.
Growth ring pattern: Transition somewhat gradual. Evenly fine textured.
Longitudinal parenchyma: Not visible with hand lens.
Rays: Fine and inconspicuous.
Miscellaneous: Odor faint but distinct and characteristically "cedary." Distinguished from western red cedar by gradual transition and differences in color and odor.

Western red cedar   *Thuja plicata*   CUPRESSACEAE

Color: Heartwood reddish or pinkish brown to dull brown, the brownish color nearly always present.
Growth ring pattern: Transition usually quite abrupt, the latewood distinct as a narrow sharply differentiated band that is noticeably denser than the latewood. Somewhat coarse textured.
Longitudinal parenchyma: Not visible with hand lens.
Rays: Narrow and inconspicuous.
Miscellaneous: Odor sweetish and aromatic.

Baldcypress   *Taxodium distichum*   TAXODIACEAE

Color: Heartwood variable, from yellow to light or dark brown or reddish. Sapwood
pale yellow.
Growth ring pattern: Transition usually abrupt. Latewood band dark and distinct.
Growth rings variable in width. Wood coarse textured.
Longitudinal parenchyma: Abundant, frequently visible with hand lens on surface
and appearing on lateral surfaces as "beaded" strands.
Rays: Relatively coarse, forming a fairly conspicuous fleck on radial surface.
Miscellaneous: Heartwood has an oily appearance and feel and, usually, a rancid
odor.

Redwood   *Sequoia sempervirens*   TAXODIACEAE

Color: Heartwood varying from light red to dark reddish brown, sapwood narrow
and whitish.
Growth ring pattern: Transition abrupt. Growth rings wide (second growth) to narrow (old growth)). Latewood narrow and dark. Wood coarse textured.
Longitudinal parenchyma: Abundant, visible with lens in sapwood and in heartwood on lateral surface as "beaded" strands.
Rays: Coarse forming a conspicuous fleck on the radial surface.
Miscellaneous: Odor distinctive to some persons. Wood is straight grained and
easily split.

REFERENCES

Anonymous. 1960. *Identification of Hardwoods—A Lens Key*. Second Edition. Forest Products Research Bulletin No. 25, Dept. of Scientific and Industrial Research, London.

Burgess, P. F. 1966. *Timbers of Sabah*. Sabah Forest Records No. 6. Forest Department, Sabah, Malaysia.

Carpenter, Charles H.; Lawrence Leney; Harold A. Core; Wilfred A. Côté, Jr.; and Arnold C. Day. 1963. *Papermaking Fibers*. State University College of Forestry at Syracuse University, Syracuse, New York. Tech. Pub. 74.

Côté, Wilfred A., Jr. 1967. *Wood Ultrastructure—An Atlas of Electron Micrographs*. University of Washington Press, Seattle.

Côté, W. A., Jr., and A. C. Day. 1969. *Wood Ultrastructure of the Southern Yellow Pines*. State University College of Forestry at Syracuse University, Syracuse, New York. Tech. Pub. 95.

Desch, H. E. 1954. *Manual of Malayan Timbers*. Vols. I & II. Malayan Forest Records No. 15. Malay Publishing House Ltd., Singapore.

Desch, H. E. 1968. *Timber, Its Structure and Properties*. Fourth Edition. St. Martins Press, New York.

Greguss, P. 1955. *Identification of Living Gymnosperms on the Basis of Xylotomy*. Akademai Kiado. Budapest, Hungary.

Harlow, W. M. 1970. *Inside Wood—Masterpiece of Nature*. American Forestry Association, Washington, D. C.

Harrar, E. S. 1957. *Hough's Encyclopedia of American Woods*. Vols. 1–13. Robert Spellers and Sons, New York.

I.A.W.A. 1964. *International Glossary of Terms Used in Wood Anatomy*. Committee on Nomenclature, International Association of Wood Anatomists. Verlagsanstalt Buchdruckerei Konkordia, Winterthur, Switzerland.

Jane, F. W. Revised by K. Wilson and D.J.B. White. 1970. *The Structure of Wood*. Second Edition. A & C Black, London.

Kollmann, F. F. P., and W. A. Côté, Jr. 1968. *Principles of Wood Science and Technology*. Vol. I, *Solid Wood*. Springer-Verlag, Berlin, New York.

Kribs, D. A. 1968. *Commercial Foreign Woods on the American Market*. Dover Publications, Inc. New York.

Little, E. L., Jr. 1953. *Check List of Native and Naturalized Trees of the United States (Including Alaska)*. Agriculture Handbook 41, Forest Service, Washington, D. C.

Metcalfe, C. R., and L. Chalk. 1950. *Anatomy of the Dicotyledons*, Vols. I & II. Oxford University Press, Amen House, London.

Meylan, B. A., and B. G. Butterfield. 1972. *Three-Dimensional Structure of Wood*. Syracuse University Press, Syracuse, New York.

Panshin, A. J., and Carl de Zeeuw. 1970. *Textbook of Wood Technology*. Volume I. Third Edition. McGraw-Hill Book Company, New York.

Phillips, E. W. J. 1948. *The Identification of Coniferous Woods by Their Microscopic Structure*. Forest Products Research Bulletin 22, London.

Record, S. J., and R. W. Hess. 1947. *Timbers of the New World*. Yale University Press, New Haven, Conn.

Tsoumis, G. 1968. *Wood as a Raw Material*. Pergamon Press, New York.

WOOD STRUCTURE AND IDENTIFICATION

was composed in VIP computerized 11-point Optima Medium and leaded two points with display type in VIP Optima Black by Dix Typesetting Co. Inc.; printed on Warren 70-pound Lustro Offset Enamel, dull, with soft covers printed on Columbia Tanalin 1700 by Vicks Lithograph and Printing Corp.; Smyth-sewn, bound over 88-pt. boards covered with Joanna French Walnut Wood Grain and GBC bound by Vail-Ballou Press, Inc.; and published by

SYRACUSE UNIVERSITY PRESS
SYRACUSE, NEW YORK